CIB PUBLISHING

Investment
Portfolio
Planning

GW00691315

Keith Popplewell ACII, APMI, MFSA

 institute of financial services

CIB Publishing
c/o The Chartered Institute of Bankers
Emmanuel House
4-9 Burgate Lane
Canterbury
Kent
CT1 2XJ
United Kingdom

Telephone: 01227 762600

CIB Publishing publications are published by The Chartered Institute of Bankers, a non-profit making registered educational charity.

The Chartered Institute of Bankers believes that the sources of information upon which the book is based are reliable and has made every effort to ensure the complete accuracy of the text. However, neither CIB, the author nor any contributor can accept any legal responsibility whatsoever for consequences that may arise from errors or omissions or any opinion or advice given.

Typeset by Kevin O'Connor
Printed by Haynes Publishing, Somerset
© Chartered Institute of Bankers 2000
ISBN 0-85297-550-3

Contents

Introduction

As with many other areas of financial planning, the range of investment options has increased significantly over the last couple of decades with new investment products being introduced almost daily, it seems. Moreover, many more areas of investment opportunities have become available to the ordinary investor which previously could be considered only by the large institutional investors; examples include investments in foreign equities and commercial property – both of which are now easily accessible through collective investment vehicles.

This increased complexity of the investment market has led on the one hand to many investors adopting (or trying to adopt) a more sophisticated approach to the planning of their portfolio, but on the other hand huge numbers of investors have become mostly or totally confused. This book is aimed at investors in both categories, aiming to demystify the portfolio planning process and strategy for the latter group of investors, and clarify and discuss apparently complex issues for those in the former category.

The book is presented in three main sections. In the first section, up to Chapter 3, we look at fundamental issues in portfolio planning (for example, the risk and reward relationship and the difference between income and capital growth-orientated assets) and key strategies in the planning process (for example, diversification). This section sets the framework of the portfolio within which the investment opportunities described and discussed in the remainder of the book may be set.

The second section (Chapters 4 to 9) looks at the main types of asset classes and discusses their relative advantages and potential disadvantages for different types of investor. These asset classes include deposit-based accounts, government bonds, equities and property (primarily commercial property). This latter category is the perfect example to illustrate the principles behind the third and final section of the book (Chapters 11 onwards): investment vehicles.

This last section considers the range of investment vehicles within which one or more of the asset classes discussed in section two may be held. Of course, certain types of asset may lend themselves to direct investment without the need for an investment vehicle – the most obvious of these being cash on deposit. Most asset classes, though, may be more profitably held within a particular vehicle, such as unit trusts, investment trusts or pension schemes. Thus the concluding chapters of this book detail and discuss the features of the main types of investment vehicle, including tax considerations, costs of trading, and any restrictions imposed by, primarily, the Inland Revenue.

Chapter 10, With-profits investments, comes after the asset class section and before the investment vehicle section. This is deliberate: we could justifiably have placed this particular form of investment, attractive to many, in either section as it is not quite an investment vehicle in itself (with-profits investments can be held only within one of the other vehicles we discuss in section three) but it is not an asset class in its own right (it is a combination of asset classes).

Overall, through these three sections, we discuss and provide guidance on strategy and content of portfolio planning and I hope you will gain enough profitable ideas and inspiration to make your portfolio planning more profitable.

1 Fundamental Principles of Investment Strategy

AN INTRODUCTION: STAGES IN CONSTRUCTING A PORTFOLIO

In this brief introductory section we suggest that fundamental stages in the construction of a portfolio for a particular investor could be :

1. Consideration of the individual needs and circumstances of the investor;
2. Identification of the most appropriate investment vehicles;
3. Identification of appropriate asset classes and sectors to be held within the selected vehicles;
4. Assessment of the expected behaviour of the portfolio over a given period of time;
5. Implementation, if the first four stages are considered appropriate by the investor;
6. Regular review of the portfolio to take account of changing individual circumstances and the performance of the constituent parts of the portfolio against the initial targets and assumptions.

These considerations will occupy our discussion through the first part of this chapter.

In the second part of the chapter we outline the main factors that help to determine the most appropriate asset classes and investment vehicles for investors in different circumstances.

CONSIDERATION OF THE INDIVIDUAL NEEDS AND CIRCUMSTANCES OF THE INVESTOR

It is neither desirable nor possible to attempt to formulate a single description of an efficient investment portfolio for all investors. Each investor enjoys (or in some cases suffers!) particular individual circumstances, for example existing investments, a balance between current income and expenditure, liability to taxation, and family circumstances. Each investor will also have his or her own plans and aspirations such as house purchase (or purchase of a larger house), early retirement, or a move abroad to work or even live permanently.

As we shall see throughout this book, each of these considerations, and many more, have a profound effect on the range of investments most suitable to each individual, and the range of investment vehicles in which those investments can most profitably be held.

It is sometimes suggested or assumed that a particular investor will have one particular need at any given point in time. This is highly unlikely to be the case, the author suggests. Take, for example, a 35-year-old married man who seeks to invest £25 per month in a regular premium investment plan but has no obvious need for the capital that would accrue: he simply wants to accumulate wealth with a very modest proportion of his earnings. He also, though, accepts the need to make adequate provision for his retirement and wants to invest £200 per month into an appropriate vehicle – a pension contract, he (perhaps prematurely) suggests. Finally, he has an existing investment portfolio of £20,000 which he views not only as an emergency fund but also as, potentially, the future financing behind his desire to eventually establish his own business. It is conceivable, is it not, that in respect of the small monthly investment plan he might be willing or even eager to adopt a high-risk profile? In respect of the more substantial accumulation of wealth within his retirement plan a less high-risk profile might be desirable, and in respect of the accumulated existing portfolio a low-risk profile might be most appropriate. Moreover, it is highly likely that different investment vehicles might be appropriate for each of these different purposes.

Thus we would suggest that, in considering an individual's needs and circumstances, each of his financial aims should be separately considered.

IDENTIFICATION OF THE MOST APPROPRIATE INVESTMENT VEHICLES

Once the investor's circumstances have been assessed, the next stage might be a consideration of the most appropriate investment *vehicle* or *vehicles* to use. To give just a few examples, a young investor wishing to make additional provision for retirement income might profitably consider the use of pension contracts, an investor seeking a suitable vehicle for routine savings and investment needs might be directed towards an Individual Savings Account (ISA), an investor not using his or her annual capital gains tax (CGT) allowances might benefit from investments in unit trusts, while an investor who is not from the United Kingdom but working here on a temporary basis might benefit from advice relating to offshore investments.

It is certainly not the intention of the strategy advocated in this book to favour any investment vehicle or vehicles over any of their alternatives. Each investment vehicle can be profitably used in particular investor circumstances, not least due to their very different structures and taxation.

Certain vehicles benefit from the availability to investors of tax relief on contributions made to those vehicles, most notably pension plans. Other vehicles benefit from favourable tax treatment on the investments held within them, such as exemption from income tax and/or capital gains tax – again we include in this category pension plans, but must also take particular note of Individual Savings Accounts (ISAs), offshore investments, and (to a lesser extent) unit trusts.

The *quid pro quo* for such tax advantageous treatment of certain vehicles is frequently the taxation liability on the investor when income or capital is withdrawn or (for example with pension plans) restrictions on when such withdrawals may be made.

Selecting appropriate investment vehicles for an investor's needs must therefore very much bear in mind the 'horses for courses' system so well accepted for so many years by horse race followers: a horse that consistently performs very well on one course may consistently underperform on other race courses.

Finally, it is not nearly so simple as even suggesting that we shall be striving to ascertain the single most appropriate investment vehicle for each investor. Many investors will have a number of investment needs and desires and it may well be the case that each of these needs is answered by a different investment vehicle.

INVESTMENT VEHICLES AND ASSET CLASSES

In the last section I briefly alluded to the principle within portfolio planning of considering investments in a number of different investment vehicles. At this stage it would be useful to clarify the terminology I shall be using throughout the rest of this book, distinguishing investment *vehicles* from investment *classes*.

Investment *asset classes* cover the range of areas in which an investment may be made either by direct purchase by the investor or indirectly through such collective investment schemes as unit trusts, investment bonds and the like. These a*sset classes* include equities, property, fixed-interest bonds, cash on deposit, and index-linked gilts. Investment *vehicles* include unit trusts, investment bonds, pension funds, investment trusts, offshore bonds and other such methods of investing in the *asset classes*.

Thus we consider the investment vehicles as being a structure in which one or more of the asset classes may be held.

IDENTIFICATION OF APPROPRIATE ASSETS CLASSES AND SECTORS TO BE HELD WITHIN THE SELECTED VEHICLES

Asset classes
After determining the more suitable investment vehicle we can then move on to a consideration of the most appropriate types of asset that may be held within that vehicle. For example, having determined that a personal pension plan may be the most suitable investment vehicle for a particular self-employed

investor, it must then be decided whether the assets to be held within that vehicle should be equity-based, fixed-interest investments, cash (or deposit-based) or any one – or more likely, a combination – of the other main asset classes.

Sectors

Even within the asset classes determined for this particular investor's investment vehicle the construction of the portfolio should give consideration to the opportunities and characteristics of different sectors within each asset class. Thus, for example, having determined that equity-based investments might be the more suitable asset to hold within the personal pension plan, it then has to be decided whether to invest in UK equities, European equities, United States equities, emerging markets, or any one of the other geographical investment areas. Further, even if it is decided to invest in UK equities there are different opportunities to invest in sectors such as banks, leisure, smaller companies, or many other different types of investment fund or strategy now widely available to investors.

Certain asset classes have particular features relating to, for example, the level of income that they produce in comparison to the expected level of capital growth, the risk and volatility inherent in that income and ongoing capital value, and the ease of investment in each asset class.

At this stage it is worth introducing the consideration (which, in fact, flows through all the aspects we have so far considered in this chapter and, indeed, the remaining considerations): the principle of risk and reward.

The relationship between investment risk and reward is fundamental to efficient portfolio planning and generally dictates that it is only by accepting higher levels of risk in an investment portfolio that an individual can hope to achieve higher levels of investment return. An investor seeking to minimize or totally avoid any risk to the underlying capital or future returns must, the theory dictates, direct the money to safe investment havens which, the investor has to accept, will yield lower returns than those that might be expected from higher-risk investments.

Nowhere is this more obvious than in considering the range of asset classes, noting with very few exceptions that the historically poorer rates of investment return have come from deposit-based savings (for example bank and building society deposit accounts) whereas the far higher investment profits have been made from stocks and shares.

It is vital, therefore, that the investor understands the nature of each asset class he or she may be considering, not only being the overall returns that might be expected in the short, medium or long term but also the risk and volatility involved during that period.

The relationship between risk and reward in investment asset classes is considered in more depth in Chapter 2, where we also consider investment strategies involving these asset classes that seek to maximize returns but minimize risk... a worthy aim indeed!

PUTTING TOGETHER THE INVESTMENT VEHICLE(S) AND THE ASSET CLASS(ES)

Unfortunately many investors have either all, or by far the largest part, of their savings tied up in only one particular investment area. This of course means that their future fortunes will depend entirely on the performance of that single investment. This can clearly not be properly described a *portfolio* because no attempt has been made to enhance investment performance, control risks, or plan investment strategies for the investor's circumstances.

Thus a fundamental principle of portfolio planning throughout this book will be to encourage investors to consider directing parts of their portfolio to a range of investment asset classes *and* investment vehicles in an attempt to truly construct an *efficient portfolio*. We are strongly suggesting, therefore, that an approach to portfolio planning concentrating solely on the selection of an appropriate mix of asset classes cannot possibly claim to fully address the investor's overall position; asset classes must be held either directly or within an investment vehicle and the most appropriate and tax advantageous method of holding those assets must be considered. The same comment and principle can be applied to an attempt to view portfolio planning as mostly or wholly a consideration of the most appropriate vehicles without addressing the mix of assets held within those vehicles.

The second part of this book looks at asset classes and sectors within those classes, without addressing (except in passing) appropriate investment vehicles. The third part then looks at appropriate vehicles but, now, starting to pick up on appropriate asset classes and sectors that may profitably be held within those vehicles. This first part of the book, though, importantly addresses some of the most important principles and strategies governing, in general terms, how an overall portfolio might or should be structured.

ASSESSMENT OF THE EXPECTED BEHAVIOUR OF THE PORTFOLIO OVER A GIVEN PERIOD OF TIME

Finally, having determined a suitable investment vehicle or vehicles (noting that, very often, an investor's portfolio will not be directed to just one vehicle) and having determined the most suitable combination of assets and asset classes, it is then necessary to 'pull it all together'.

Although by this stage we are well on the way to constructing an efficient investment portfolio, great care has to be taken to balance the different investment vehicles and asset classes used for each investor and so we must now 'bring it all together' by defining, or attempting to define, for the suggested portfolio the level of returns and the level of risk expected from each individual investment made within the portfolio. Furthermore, and arguably most importantly, the *overall* returns and risk from the combined portfolio should be defined.

It should not be assumed that the total returns and risk of a portfolio is simply the sum of the returns and risk from the constituent parts of the portfolio: as we shall discuss in Chapter 3 one of the most important aims of efficient portfolio planning is to maximize investment returns while minimizing investment risk. It is important to be able to expect that the future behaviour of the portfolio as a whole should often be more readily and accurately determinable than the behaviour of a constituent part of that portfolio. This, with proper portfolio planning, can be facilitated by due consideration being given to the principles of diversification and, in particular, correlation strategy. This latter strategy is considered in greater detail in Chapter 3, indicating primarily that certain combinations of types of asset should behave in broadly similar ways to each other whereas other combinations of assets can be expected to behave very differently from each other.

IMPLEMENTATION

Here we pay some attention to the actual implementation of the strategy for a investor's portfolio, including details of exactly how, where, and through whom the investment can and should be made.

Having finally determined the constituent parts of a desired portfolio the investor must now ascertain how best to put this plan into effect.

In this respect the investor must choose whether to make each individual investment personally, corresponding with the investment vehicle or asset class provider directly, or nominate an intermediary to effect such investments on his or her behalf – possibly having already given the investor advice relating to one or more of those investments or, indeed, the portfolio as a whole. The range of intermediaries may be confusing for some investors and includes the financial services arms of banks and building societies as well as independent financial advisers, insurance company representatives, stockbrokers, accountants and solicitors.

It is not the intention of the author, and certainly not within this book, to guide or direct investors to any particular category of intermediary except where (rarely) certain investments may be made or may best be made only through one particular route: in these circumstances the author will not hesitate to give definitive guidance.

REVIEW

Furthermore, within this implementation strategy we pay attention to the need for regular reviews of the portfolio to ensure that its make-up on an ongoing basis matches the ongoing circumstances and needs of the investor.

The construction of an efficient investment portfolio can be a difficult and time-consuming task, particularly where an investor has numerous and complex needs. It is therefore tempting to implement the final strategy with some relief. This relief, for many, is unfortunately then followed by many months or years of investment inactivity, trusting that the initial portfolio strategy will hold good forever.

Rarely, though, should portfolios remain static. Investors' needs and circumstances change, for example an individual who was liable to income tax at only the basic rate may progress to become a higher rate taxpayer and the preferred investment vehicles within a portfolio will change dramatically at that time. Moreover, an individual's attitude to investment risk might change dramatically as, perhaps, the spendable income increases from a mere subsistence level to being able to enjoy a comfortable level of surplus income over expenditure. As a final example, though many others could be listed, an investor's future plans might change dramatically – an investor may have expressed a desire and intention to live abroad permanently in the not-too-distant future, but if this desire changes then so will the recommendation for the most appropriate investment vehicles (probably moving away from offshore investments towards more conventional onshore investments).

It might, though, not only be the investor's circumstances and future outlook that change, the features and outlook for individual investment vehicles and asset classes can change dramatically from one year to the next. As an example, the removal of the right of pension schemes to reclaim Advance Corporation Tax (ACT) withheld by the company on paying dividends could be seen as detrimentally effecting the outlook for investments in pension funds (as a *vehicle*) and also the attractions of equity investing generally (as an asset class).

Over the last decade or so the rates of return available from deposit-based investments and those from fixed-interest investments have fallen significantly and, along with the huge fall in inflation within the UK and across the world generally over the last couple of decades, the outlook for many different classes of asset has changed dramatically.

Therefore it is important to monitor the progress of an investment portfolio, setting target rates of income and growth over different time periods and subsequently comparing actual performance against these targets, adjusting the portfolio where appropriate to take account of the changing investment markets and the respective performances of different asset classes. This review, which should take place no less frequently than annually, must also include, as briefly discussed above, a consideration of any changes within the investor's circumstances (tax position, financial position etc.) and/or his or her changing aspirations and plans. Without such a review the investor could soon find that the portfolio, which had every prospect initially of working efficiently for present needs, soon becomes out-dated and almost totally inappropriate to the circumstances.

FACTORS IN DETERMINING APPROPRIATE VEHICLES AND ASSET CLASSES FOR A PARTICULAR INVESTOR

The term 'investor' includes a wide range of individuals, companies, pension schemes, trusts, charities and other bodies who have spare capital that is not required for immediate use.

In this book we shall be considering only individuals – or families – as investors, although this will include individuals (and their families) investing through such vehicles as trusts and pension schemes which, although these vehicles could be considered on the one hand as 'investors' in their own right, are treated here as investment vehicles.

The factors we shall be looking at are:

– risk profile and expected returns;
– income and capital needs of the investor – now and in the future;
– tax position of the investor.

RISK PROFILE AND EXPECTED RETURNS

There is an acknowledged and fundamental relationship – not only in investment planning, but also in many other aspects of life – between risk and reward. Individuals prepared (or even seeking) to accept higher levels of risk in their portfolio will, the theory dictates, generally be rewarded with higher rewards in the longer term. In the meantime, though, they will have to tolerate greater fluctuations in the value of their investments.

The dilemma for investors therefore appears to be that, in search of higher returns they will have to accept higher risk and this is, indeed, the perceived wisdom. With no understanding or knowledge of portfolio planning, this perceived wisdom is usually also a truism, but there would be little point offering a book such as this if the purpose were only to explain or prove these accepted concepts.

We therefore seek to demonstrate throughout this book that it may be possible to achieve the highest rates of investment return with the lowest degrees of risk – not by investing in one single asset or investment vehicle but by combining different asset classes and vehicles in such a way as to be able to realistically expect above-average returns with below-average risk and volatility. These strategies are outlined and discussed in more detail in Chapter 3.

INCOME AND CAPITAL NEEDS OF THE INVESTOR – NOW AND IN THE FUTURE

Structuring an appropriate portfolio for an investor must take into account that individual's income needs, both now and in the future. Certain investments may be highly efficient, especially as regards taxation, but if they provide, say, only capital gains with little access to the underlying capital in the short term they may not be appropriate for an investor requiring a high level of income from the portfolio.

Similar consideration must be given to the investor's need or desire to produce, or make available, a capital sum at a known or unknown point in the future.

By considering, together, the balance between the investor's income and capital growth requirements it is possible to identify indicators to particular types of asset and particular investment vehicles most likely to satisfy the investor's overall requirements.

TAX POSITION OF THE INVESTOR

A crucial aspect of portfolio planning involves consideration of the investor's taxation position, as regards income tax, capital gains tax (CGT) and inheritance tax (IHT). Various types of investment and investment vehicle can be identified as being particularly appropriate to those paying income tax at the basic rate, or at the higher rate, or indeed not liable to income tax at all. Other investment options may be attractive to individuals who are fully utilizing their annual CGT allowance or those who are not using this allowance. Finally, investors with a potential liability to IHT should attempt to plan their portfolio not only in such a way as to minimize income tax and CGT liability, but also to minimize future IHT liability – or at the very least not increase such liability. A little more detail on these points is noted below, with a few examples, but much more discussion and detail of these points forms a fundamental core aspect of the remaining chapters in this book.

Income Tax

Higher-rate taxpayers should generally look for investments that are exempt from liability to income tax. These include certain forms of National Savings and pension contracts (which, indeed, benefit from tax relief on contributions as well as income tax exemption on the growth in the pension fund). As regards National Savings vehicles, however, the higher-rate taxpayer will typically find that he or she has to accept a relatively mediocre rate of return – not coincidentally of course, but in recognition of the tax-free status of the investment.

Non-taxpayers should not concern themselves with tax exemption but should, quite simply, look for the highest *gross* rate of return.

Definition: Gross

Where an investment declares *gross* returns – either in the form of income or as capital growth – these returns will be paid without deduction of tax by the investment provider. However, these returns are liable to income tax and so the investor must (or at least *should!*) declare them to the Inland Revenue. Tax is then levied on the investor, usually through his or her tax code though frequently by separate payments to the Inland Revenue.

Basic-rate taxpayers fall somewhere between these two extremes of taxpayers. There are no specific examples of investments that stand out as being more suitable for basic-rate taxpayers than for the other two categories we have briefly considered above.

An important consideration should be borne in mind with regard to taxable investment income: an investor may be a non-taxpayer on his or her existing income but with the addition of further taxable investment income could move into the lower-rate tax band or, indeed (if the taxable investment income is so substantial), even in the basic-rate income tax band. If this looks likely then the investor should pay particular attention to try to restrict taxable investment income, perhaps preferring instead investments that give rise to capital gains (thereby taking advantage of CGT allowances). Similar considerations apply to basic-rate taxpayers whose income is only marginally below the level at which they will be liable to higher-rate tax.

All taxpayers should take care not to consider only *their own* liability to income tax but also the liability to tax within any investment vehicle they may consider. As an example, although *investment bonds* can be highly attractive to some investors, as we discuss later in this book, they suffer a tax on income and gains – internally, within the bond – that cannot be reclaimed by non-taxpayers who, therefore, should usually look at alternative investment vehicles that allow the investor to be entirely liable for income tax. The taxation of investment vehicles is discussed throughout this book, in the relevant chapters.

Capital Gains Tax (CGT)
It is an unfortunate fact that many taxpayers do not give sufficient thought to structuring their investments in such a way as to make use of their annual exemption from CGT. They accept liability to income tax on their portfolio without giving fuller consideration to investments and investment vehicles that give rise to a liability to CGT rather than to income tax.

The vast majority of investors are liable to pay income tax, but the vast majority of those people come nowhere near to using up all of their annual CGT allowance and so miss investment opportunities where a theoretical liability to tax on profits (CGT) is avoided by offsetting those profits against the annual exemption.

We pay particular attention in this book, in part two (asset classes) and part three (investment vehicles), to investments that give rise to a CGT liability rather than an income tax liability, and we would urge investors to pay particular attention to this aspect of portfolio planning.

THE PROGRESSION OF THE CHAPTERS IN THIS BOOK

The flow of the book broadly follows the flow of the considerations outlined in this chapter. At the conclusion of each section within the book we look at a selection of particular investment strategies that may be appropriate to investors in certain circumstances.

2 Values and Market Prices of Assets, Investment Returns, and Interrelationships between Asset Classes

INTRODUCTION

When investors look at the range of assets and investment vehicles open to consideration within a portfolio they could be forgiven for thinking that the price at which they can buy and sell those assets, and the rate of return they can expect from those assets, is largely arbitrary. This is most definitely not true. Although actual returns from individual investments frequently fail to match expectations – either in surplus or deficit – it is nonetheless important for potential investors to be able to determine at the outset what returns – income and capital growth – could reasonably be anticipated. This, in turn, relies on the investor being able to identify the factors that affect the value and eventual returns from investments.

Once this appreciation is grasped the investor can then move on to structuring a portfolio around combinations of investment vehicles and assets that are *most likely* to produce, among other things, the combined level of risk and reward required for particular circumstances and purpose or purposes.

We therefore, in this chapter, consider the concepts of *supply and demand* and *risk and reward* which then permit us to attempt to quantify, for a given investment opportunity, *relative value*. I would like to stress, at this stage, that these concepts, as with almost every other investment concept, can claim to do no more than give an indication of relative values of investments; they do not even pretend to identify provable mathematical and market values. Other factors come into play in determining market prices from day to day, as we shall discuss.

SUPPLY AND DEMAND

Market prices of investments do not happen by accident. They depend on the fundamental relationship between supply and demand. If demand increases without supply matching that increase, the price of the investment will rise: there are more potential investors wanting to buy than there are existing holders ready to sell. To tempt those holders to sell buyers must increase the price they are prepared to pay. Just how great that increase has to be depends on the scale of the imbalance between supply and demand.

It is crucial for an investor to understand this relationship, and the consequence on investment yields of an increase in the market price of an investment.

Supply and demand, a simple example – fixed-interest investments

If a long-term fixed-interest investment offers an annual income of £10 at a market price of £100 (thus a yield of 10%) at a time when comparative investments also offer a similar yield it is clear that this investment is reasonably priced at this time. If subsequently market yields suddenly fall to 5%, the fixed-interest yield in question will look exceptionally attractive and demand would far outstrip supply. The market price would rise sharply, in fact to such a level that the equivalent yield once again represents fair competitive value. In fact, it can be seen that the market price would rise to £200, at which price the yield equates to 5% (that is, the fixed annual income of £10 expressed as a percentage of the new market price of £200). At this new price the market in the investment remains in a state of equilibrium: the level of demand equates to the level of supply, primarily taking into account yield available on alternative investments.

In practice other factors must be taken into account, as we shall discuss when we consider individual investments in more detail, but this simple example should illustrate that the conditions of supply and demand change frequently, and that for most investment classes there is a relationship between the price of the asset and the effective yield an investor achieves on buying or holding that asset.

RELATIVE VALUE

We have so far looked at the concepts of supply and demand, and of risk and reward, and their combined effect in arriving at the prices of assets and the yields available from those assets. But both of these two fundamental relationships are 'movable feasts', by which I mean that additional, or reduced, supply or demand for a particular investment can materialize for many reasons. One reason is, of course, the movement in market interest/investment yields generally, but many other possible factors can come into play from time to time, just a small number of which are outlined below for illustration purposes (although many more will be highlighted throughout the book when we look at each asset in more detail).

Regulatory influences
Final-salary pension schemes have in recent years been required to certify that the value and security of their assets are – and will continue to be for the foreseeable future – sufficient to match their projected liabilities (i.e. pensions and death benefits payable to members and beneficiaries). This requirement is known as the Minimum Funding Requirement (MFR) and (in effect) attaches a greater degree of perceived value to certain assets than others: fixed-interest government bonds are deemed lower risk than equities. Where an asset is deemed higher risk, the scheme may not take all of the current market value into account anticipating (in effect) a possible fall in market values. Schemes must therefore hold higher amounts than would otherwise be the case in investments rated (at least implicitly) as 'higher risk' and so, understandably, demand from these buyers increased for 'safe investments'. This increased demand for fixed-interest government bonds – which in this respect had

17

nothing to do with prevailing market interest rates or any change in the perceived risk of this investment – caused upwards pressure on the market price.

Structural change in a particular market

During the 1980s and, more particularly, the early 1990s the value of commercial property was frequently volatile (see the definition of volatility, below). Property prices depended on market forces, true, as measured by specialist valuers.

However, commercial investment property has increasingly – especially since the early 1990s – come to be valued more according to the rental income it yields than according to any theoretical bricks-and-mortar assessment. By this I mean that commercial property rental income yields have generally been running for the last five or six years at around 8%: a property yielding rent of £80,000 per annum – if let on a good lease to a good quality tenant – has a market price of £1 million. It does not matter so much what a theoretical 'bricks-and-mortar' value is given to the property: the main value is in the rental yield (and quality of lease). This being the case, where a property is let on a long-term lease to good quality tenants the value of the property cannot fluctuate wildly because the rental yield is secure and predictable (frequently, predictably upwards according to the terms of each lease). Thus commercial investment property prices have over recent years markedly reduced in volatility and, if this continues, one would expect those prices to rise sharply if and when the market as a whole accepts this assessment of the fundamental structural change in the investment property market.

RISK AND REWARD

The concept of the relationship between the level of risk one accepts, or perhaps seeks, from an investment and the long-term rewards that might consequently be expected is widely acknowledged and understood. The higher the relative returns required, the higher the level of risk that has to be accepted.

This relationship does not happen by accident, it happens by market forces.

Risk and return – an example of how market forces maintain the relationship

If the fixed-interest asset we used in our earlier example, yielding 10% at a market price of £100, offers that rate of future return but with an identifiable level of risk (to the yield or to the capital value, or both) yet a very similar investment opportunity offered a yield of only 5% totally free of risk, we have already seen that we would expect the price of the first asset to double to bring the yields comparable at 5% (either that, or the price of the second asset would halve in value). However, with both – similar – assets now yielding 5% an investor would be foolish, would he not, to consider the first asset, which simply means that he will be taking a higher level of risk but with no greater reward. The price of that first asset must fall (or the price of the second asset rise) to return these two assets to fair comparative value. The price will fall by, say, 10% if the additional perceived risk is 10% (a simplification, but one that will suffice for this stage in the book): at £180 – rather than £200 – the £10 fixed-interest payment represents a yield of around 5.5% – a higher yield than the safe investment but with a higher degree of risk.

Thus the market will by the process of supply and demand arrive at a price for each investment that reflects its combined perception of that asset's level of risk.

A concept very closely related to that of risk is volatility: the latter aspect relating more to very short-term fluctuations in value and income returns whereas the former concept (risk) is generally used to describe the longer-term risk to capital and income returns.

VOLATILITY

The principle of investment *risk* is commonly defined as the chances that, over a period of time, the average rate of return will exceed a stipulated percentage – usually termed the critical yield in certain aspects of investment planning within pension contracts – in order that a particular strategy might work in the investor's favour. Hence, for example, a pension income drawdown illustration might show that an investor's invested fund needs to achieve an average annual rate of return of, say, 8.5% if drawdown is to prove financially profitable over a conventional annuity purchase. A lower average annual rate of return than 8.5% will, it is thereby surmised, result in the investor being financially disadvantaged, while a higher rate than 8.5% will result in financial gain.

In isolation, though, the average rate of return can reveal only half of the investment risk (and reward) picture: volatility is the other half.

The concept of volatility can be explained in outline by taking an exaggerated example.

Example

Fred, aged 60, retires with a personal pension fund of £100,000 after taking tax-free cash, and transfers this fund to a drawdown contract, taking the maximum permitted income of £10,000 per annum.

Unfortunately for Fred in the first year his investment fund falls by 50% and so, after taking his £10,000 income withdrawal, he has only £40,000 remaining in his fund after just twelve months.

In the second year his investment fund unfortunately falls in value by a further 40%, leaving him with only £14,000 at the end of year two after taking into account his £10,000 withdrawal.

In year three Fred sees his fund fall a further 20% which, after taking into account his £10,000 withdrawal, leaves him with only a little over £1,000 at the end of this third year. At this point, his contract is of course due its first triennial review.

Continuing this extreme scenario, we will now assume investment performance to improve somewhat over the following years, although not nearly enough to permit Fred to take anywhere near the level of income he enjoyed for the first three years (or, indeed, he would have been enjoying had he chosen a conventional annuity purchase).

Then, in the year of his 71st birthday, his investment fund grows in value by a staggering 500%... but, by this time, Fred had only 2p remaining (not, we have to stress, a scientifically-calculated value for this example) in his fund at the start of the year and this consequently grows to 12p (although it still does not, of course, permit withdrawal of any meaningful level of income).

In the following year (Fred's aged 72) investment performance once more enjoys staggering growth – this time of 400% – but, when applied to the remaining fund of only 12p, still gives him a fund of only 60p in total and again no possibility of withdrawal of income. This phenomenal growth continues until he reaches age 75 but, because of the low base, his total accumulated fund is a meagre £14.78 (again, a 'made up number' simply for illustration purposes) with which to buy a conventional annuity!

In these circumstances it is no surprise that Fred complains, claiming he has been given bad advice. His financial adviser revisits the original file only to discover that the original illustration indicated that an average rate of growth in excess of 8% should have made the drawdown strategy profitable. Adding up each year's investment gains in percentage terms, deducting losses and then dividing the total by the number of years of the contract, the adviser arrives at an average annual return over the fifteen-year period of, say, 20%. This high average has arisen because there were some very high investment gains towards the end of the drawdown contract term, more than counterbalancing the losses during the early years.

Nevertheless, in spite of the apparently high average investment return it is indisputable that the drawdown strategy has failed in this instance: Fred has been able to enjoy only an extremely small level of income withdrawal (even without taking charges into account) throughout the last ten years of the fifteen-year contract term and now retains only a negligible fund with which to buy a conventional annuity.

So what has gone wrong? Clearly, the losses in the early years, especially when coupled with a high level of withdrawals, make it impossible for gains in the later years – even dramatic gains – to compensate.

THE DIFFERENCE BETWEEN AVERAGE RATES OF RETURN AND VOLATILITY

Average rates of return give, quite simply, a snapshot summary of the overall fund performance over a given period of time. Volatility, in contrast, shows

21

for the same investment fund how bad or good the performance may have been from time to time.

RISK AND REWARD, AND AN INTRODUCTION TO THE MEASUREMENT OF VOLATILITY

It is a well-understood principle of investment that risk and reward almost invariably go hand-in-hand: the greater the desired reward (rate of investment growth) the greater the level of risk the investor must accept.

For example, over a longer term the returns on equities have far outstripped the returns from Government bonds which, in turn, have far exceeded the returns from cash deposits. Looking to the future there is little doubt that an investor has a greater chance of suffering a loss of a significant part of his capital by investing in equities as opposed to investing in gilts (at least over the short term) and a greater chance of a loss in a gilt investment than by putting money on deposit. The greater potential investment reward from equities is possible only by accepting a greater level of risk – particularly in the shorter term. In short, equity values are generally more volatile than gilt prices which, in turn, are generally more volatile than returns on deposits. But how can we measure the volatility of investment returns?

STANDARD DEVIATIONS

Standard deviations seek to give an indication of just how far away from an average rate of return the actual investment return might deviate over any given period, with the standard deviation being measured over a historical period of years.

The measurement of one standard deviation shows how far the investment performance has deviated from the average over approximately 70% of the period in question.

An example might be helpful.

Example – Fund A

If we are looking at Fund A's investment performance over, say, the last 20 years to find that the average annual gain has been calculated as 9%, we might also note (from providers of investment performance statistics) that the standard deviation has been 4. What does that number '4' indicate? It indicates that in 70% of the years under review the investment return has never been lower than 4% below the average rate of return nor higher than 4% above the average rate of return. Thus, in 14 years out of the 20 years under review (i.e. 70% of the time) the annual rate of return to an investor has neither fallen below 5% (i.e. the average of 9% less the standard deviation of 4) nor been higher than 13% (i.e. the average of 9% plus the standard deviation of 4).

At this stage we do not know either the lowest rate of return the investor will have suffered, or the highest rate from which he or she benefited during the other 30% of the time (because the definition of one standard deviation covers only 70% of the time). We shall return to this in a short while.

Would an investor consider that particular fund – with an average rate of return of 9% and a standard deviation of 4 – to be volatile? The next question to ask must be: 'volatile compared to what?'

Let us make a comparison with another example investment fund:

Example – Fund B

Fund B has grown over the last 20 years by an average of 11% per annum and we are told it has a standard deviation over that period of 16. This means that in 70% of the years under review – again, 14 years out of 20 – the investor could have suffered a loss of up to 5% of the fund (i.e. the average gain of 11% less the standard deviation of 16 which gives a minus number in this case) but may have enjoyed an investment gain of up to 27% (this being the average rate of return of 11% plus the standard deviation of 16).

Comparing the two investments we can see not only that Fund B's average rate of return is higher than that of Fund A, but also that the volatility of Fund B is higher and brings with it, in some years, the increased potential for higher losses or higher gains than might be suffered or enjoyed by Fund A.

23

From these examples you should be able to clearly identify that the higher the standard deviation of an investment the higher has been its volatility (noting again that the standard deviations are usually calculated on a historical basis and may not necessarily be an accurate guide to future performance).

VOLATILITY AND AN INVESTOR'S PREFERRED INVESTMENT STRATEGY

Higher volatility, it should be stressed, does not indicate an inferior investment – simply that the investor might expect wider fluctuations in investment returns from one year to the next.

Some investors actively seek higher volatile funds in the expectation over the longer period of higher average rates of return (the risk and reward relationship again), whereas other investors want desperately to avoid fluctuating returns.

TWO STANDARD DEVIATIONS

So far we have assessed only what has happened to the investment return 70% of the time – the definition of one standard deviation. But what about the investment performance the other 30% of the time?

It may therefore be useful to look at the figure for two standard deviations, which explains how far from the average an investment has deviated during approximately 95% of the time.

Example – Fund A
With an average annual rate of return of 9% and one standard deviation of 4, we now discover that the figure for two standard deviations is 7. This means that during 70% of the time the investment return has

deviated no more than 4% from the average (giving an annual rate of return between 5% and 13%) and during 95% of the time has deviated no more that 7% away from the average – showing that only rarely (5% of the time) has the annual rate of return been lower than 2% (9% minus 7%) and no higher than 16% (9% plus 7%). In other words, when the investment return has fallen outside the relatively narrow range covered by one standard deviation (70% of the time) it has not done so by much (although you should note that we still do not know what has happened to fund performance for the remaining 5% of the period in question).

Example – Fund B

With the average annual rate of return 11% we have already noted that during 70% of the time the returns in any year would not have been lower than -5%, or higher than +27% (one standard deviation being 16). If we are now told that the measure for two standard deviations of Fund B is 30, this means that during 95% of the time the annual rate of return has been as low as -19% (11% minus 30%) but could have been as high as +41% (11% + 30%). This is further indication that Fund B has been much more volatile over the last 20 years than Fund A. Whether it is likely to remain so can be indicated by looking at its current declared investment strategy, among other factors.

ONE AND TWO STANDARD DEVIATIONS – A SUMMARY

By looking at the measure of one standard deviation and two standard deviations we can arrive at a useful assessment of how investment returns have deviated away from the average most of the time (70% – one deviation) and almost all of the time (95% – two standard deviations).

DEVISING INVESTMENT STRATEGIES USING STANDARD DEVIATIONS

How can the concept of standard deviations help in devising an investment strategy and advising the investor of potential risks? Even a small amount of thought should provide an answer to this question. We are now able to indicate to investors – albeit only from a historical perspective – 'how bad did it get?' and 'how good did it get?' before, if required, selecting investments that are likely to restrict the investor's down-side risk to a level acceptable to his or her requirements.

With cash deposits at the lower end of likely investment returns but also at the lower end of volatility, and with equities at the higher end both in terms of potential returns and volatility, the recommended investment strategy is crucial – not least to a pension drawdown decision.

There are investment analysis techniques that seek to predict future standard deviations for different asset classes (e.g. equities, property, deposit, gilts), although these can never claim the precision of historic measurements and are beyond the scope of this book.

Measurements of volatility are therefore an important aspect of portfolio planning, which should be utilized just as frequently as average historical or expected rates of return. They can, furthermore, be profitably utilized in certain specific investment portfolio strategies, as we shall discuss in the next chapter.

PRICING INFLUENCES – A SUMMARY

In this chapter we have considered in some depth the main influences that drive the prices of, and returns from, different classes of assets and sectors within those classes. We strongly suggest that an appreciation of the relative values of different assets at a given point in time and an informed assessment of the likely future performance of those assets can be achieved only by an understanding of these pricing influences.

Throughout the remainder of this book, therefore, and certainly throughout the second part of the book (in which we assess the main asset classes) the most important of these influences, where appropriate, will be referred to and developed.

3 Investment Strategies – An Introduction

INTRODUCTION

Quite apart from determining suitable asset classes and investment vehicles for an individual investor, the way in which they may be combined within a portfolio to give enhanced overall investment returns and/or reduced overall portfolio risk and volatility is, of course, extremely important.

In this chapter we look at a number of the most important and/or most discussed strategies in this respect, directing our attentions at both lump-sum ('one-off') investments and regular – or at least periodic – contributions to a portfolio. The three particular strategies (a number of smaller concepts are contained in each strategy) are:

- diversification;
- correlation; and
- efficient frontier.

COMBINING CONCEPTS AND STRATEGIES

As we have already noted in the previous chapters it is a fundamental concept of investment theory that risk and reward go hand in hand. If an investor wants to reduce or avoid risk in a portfolio, so the theory goes, he or she must invest in low-risk assets. But, given the choice, almost *everybody* wants to invest in low-risk assets and so this pushes up the price of those assets, or reduces the pressure on the provider of those assets to pay attractive returns.

Either way, low-risk assets almost invariably come hand-in-hand with low (or comparatively low) returns. Only those who take risks with their investment can expect, we have traditionally been led to believe (with justification), above average investment rewards.

This leaves us in a quandary, when planning a portfolio, as to where the balance lies between an acceptably low level of risk and an acceptably high level of investment return. However, in this chapter we look at investment strategies that seek to yield high levels of portfolio return, usually associated only with high-risk investments, by combining a series of high-risk/high-reward individual investments in such a way as to create a low-risk profile to the overall portfolio.

The best of both worlds – a portfolio offering high returns with low risk? Perhaps. This is not simply a theoretical and unachievable aim but, as you will see throughout this chapter, a practical and workable strategy that will add value to any investment portfolio. The strategy builds upon three main principles, developing the concept of volatility, discussed in the last chapter: *diversification*, *correlation strategy*, and the definition of an *efficient frontier*.

DIVERSIFICATION

If all an investor's money rests in shares in just one company on the stock market – for example, HSBC Bank plc – then the value of the portfolio (which cannot really be called a portfolio, with no diversification, of course) relies completely on the behaviour of HSBC's share price. Diversification would, as can clearly be appreciated even with no technical knowledge of portfolio planning, reduce the level of portfolio risk: the investor should sell some HSBC shares and buy a mixture of other shares.

Can we quantify the reduction in risk, within the portfolio, of diversification?
To some extent, yes. There is a mathematical investment concept, in this connection, called *portfolio size and residual risk*, a summary of which appears in the table over the page:

PORTFOLIO SIZE	RESIDUAL RISK (%)
1	100
2	50
4	25
5	20
10	10
20	5
25	4
50	2
100	1
1,000	0.1

You can, I am sure, see that this is not a 'rocket science' concept. It suggests that diversifying between, say, two investments within the portfolio ('portfolio science') will reduce the overall risk ('residual risk') to 50% of what it would have been had the entire portfolio been invested in just one investment. Spreading the portfolio between four assets reduces the residual risk to 25%, and so on.

Whether or not we agree with the strict mathematics behind this concept we can, I am sure, generally agree with the underlying theory. Or can we?

WHEN MIGHT PORTFOLIO DIVERSIFICATION NOT WORK?

Or, to be more precise, in what circumstances might diversification not reduce the overall risk profile of the portfolio as much as we would hope?

Suppose the investor, currently with all his 'portfolio' in HSBC shares, accepts a suggestion that diversification can reduce portfolio risk and sells, say, 80% of the shares. He or she then invests the proceeds as follows:

20%   remains invested in HSBC
20%   Lloyds TSB Bank

20%   Barclays Bank
20%   Royal Bank of Scotland
20%   Halifax Bank

Has he or she reduced the risk in his portfolio?

Not really. He or she *has* reduced the risk of HSBC shares doing particularly badly but, clearly, *has not* reduced the risk of high street banks, as a sector, performing badly. If HSBC does badly, it will usually be because of adverse sentiment to the whole of the banking sector. This might be because of interest rate movements, regulatory threats to an important profit earning part of their business, or any other sector-specific considerations that might affect the demand for shares in this sector. The poor performance might, of course, relate specifically to HSBC shares (perhaps after having made a particularly unsuccessful foray into ownership of an American bank) but usually the trend in the HSBC share price will reflect the trend in bank share prices generally.

Of course, the share prices of banks have not always mirrored each other, but for the largest part of the time the trend in their share price performance has been very close. This similarity in performance, in portfolio planning terminology, leads to an assessment that the two shares have been *highly correlated.*

DIVERSIFICATION BETWEEN EQUITY SECTORS IN THE UK

How great would have been the reduction in risk of the portfolio if the investor had diversified, away from HSBC , 50% to Barclays? Not much. What happens to HSBC share price generally also happens to Barclays, and vice-versa of course.

This is not only true of the banking sector, but also of most other stock market sectors: the share price of one water board (e.g. Anglian Water) could be expected to closely mirror the share price of most of the other water boards (Severn Trent, Thames, etc.) not least because of the pressures (or otherwise) from OFWAT, their regulator. Many other examples can be identified in other sectors.

So, diversification away from shares in HSBC to shares in other high street banks avoids the specific risk in HSBC but it does not avoid the risk of the high street banking sector performing badly.

Diversification between different *sectors* could, then, achieve a greater reduction in portfolio risk. The investor might decide, therefore, to direct the proceeds of his HSBC Bank share sales in, say, a company from the chemicals sector, one from the building sector, one from the retail sector, and so on. But does this diversification between the sectors satisfactorily remove or substantially reduce the overall risk profile of his portfolio? Not really. It removes the specific HSBC Bank risk and even the banking sector risk but it does not remove the more general risk of the UK stock market as a whole.

Although different sectors within the UK equity market frequently move in different directions at any particular point in time nonetheless a *sustained* upward trend in UK share prices will tend to benefit the majority of shares across all the sectors (and conversely a sustained downward trend tends to hit the vast majority of shares).

An illustration of these points is noted below, showing the *Financial Times* index of a number of sectors within UK equities over a one-year period to the end of 1999:

> Information and technology shares rose 435%
> Software and computing services rose 131%
> Mining shares rose 126%

On the other hand:

> Food producers and processors lost 28%
> Personal care and household products lost 28%
> Tobacco lost 31%

It is also instructive to note not only the fluctuations between the different sectors but also the variations between the price performance of the different *sizes* of companies ('sizes', here, being defined by their market capitalization – i.e. the total value of all the company's shares). This particular issue is developed more fully in Chapter 9 but, briefly, an initial assessment might be useful here. An extract from the *Financial Times* index, again up to the end of 1999 shows:

The FTSE 100 Index (the largest 100 quoted shares, by capitalization) rose 14%
The FTSE 250 Index (the largest 250 shares, obviously including the FTSE 100 Shares) rose 30%
The FTSE 'Small Capitalization' (the smallest quoted companies) rose 44%.

This was, clearly, a good year for shares in smaller companies, especially shares in smaller companies in the information technology field. It was a less good year, though, for the very largest companies – in particular the very largest tobacco companies (mostly because of USA law suits, as it happens) and those in the business of food production and processing (not least because of health scares and increasing competition among retailers driving down prices and profit margins).

However, share prices are notoriously or reliably cyclical (the viewpoint depends on how well the portfolio is planned to take these fluctuations into account, and profit by them). In the following year the investor should be under no doubt that 'what goes up must come down' or 'the bigger they are the harder they fall' or whatever other metaphor one cares to quote to explain the fact that no asset can continue to outperform the market in the longer term: last year's glory shares frequently become this year's *bête noire*.

We can and should therefor develop this idea of diversification, not just away from HSBC Bank specifically, and away from the banking sector, and now even away from UK shares: portfolio risk could and should be further reduced if we take a global approach to our equity portfolio.

EQUITY DIVERSIFICATION AWAY FROM THE UK

Notwithstanding the evidence above, that not all shares or sectors in the UK behave in exactly the same way at the same time, nonetheless it is a truism that a general upward or downward trend in UK share prices will tend to have an impact on most UK shares.

Therefore an equity portfolio consisting entirely of UK equities reduces risk by diversification between sectors that are not highly correlated, but does not reduce the risk that UK equities in general may fall.

Further risk reduction in an equity portfolio may therefore be achieved by directing part of the portfolio to equities in other countries. However, it can be identified that diversification overseas may not significantly reduce the overall portfolio risk if that diversification takes place to the equities in a country whose stock market performance is highly correlated with the UK's stock market performance – the USA being a prime example of this. European stock markets have been quite highly correlated with the UK's, although not to the same degree as the USA correlation. Far East stock markets have had a lower correlation with the UK than either the USA or Europe.

Where does this all lead us? Simply, remember, that diversification between highly correlated investments means that they will usually behave in the same way at the same time and, this being the case, the overall risk or volatility of the portfolio will not be significantly reduced. Diversification, where designed to reduce portfolio risk, will be more effective between investments with a low correlation.

DIVERSIFICATION BETWEEN CLASSES OF ASSET

We can, and should, take this idea of diversification beyond a consideration only of equities.

Although we can identify world stock markets that are lowly, or quite lowly, correlated with each other we can nonetheless identify trends which show that, over the long term in particular, most countries' stock markets will tend to rise and fall in tandem. Therefore even the most diversified, low-correlated, portfolio of equities cannot substantially remove the overall risk of equities in the longer term.

The investor should, therefore, seriously consider diversification into other asset classes such as government bonds (gilts), property (probably through pooled funds), corporate bonds (again, probably through pooled funds), and deposit-based investments (cash).

Now, some of these asset classes are themselves highly correlated. Take, for example, fixed-interest gilts and corporate bonds. Although issued by different organizations (the former by the government, the latter by companies) they are very similar in nature and behaviour, both being fixed-interest investments. Thus diversification between these two asset classes would not materially reduce the risk or volatility profile of the portfolio. However, equities and commercial property have for many years been lowly correlated, indicating that diversification between these two asset classes *will* reduce the risk profile of the portfolio.

However, identifying asset classes that are lowly correlated with each other, although reducing the risk profile of the portfolio, may tempt the investor into asset classes that offer poor returns – whether income or growth. A highly diversified low correlated portfolio is little use if the total returns are poor.

This leads us to the main principle of correlation theory: combining 'high performance' investments (which are individually usually highly volatile) within a portfolio to achieve overall high performance returns but with a much reduced risk and volatility profile. 'Low-performance' investments are generally to be avoided as a means of reducing the portfolio risk. This is known as *correlation strategy.*

CORRELATION STRATEGY

Over each of the next seven chapters I would therefore urge you to take particular notice of a short but very important section in which we progressively look at the correlation between all the main asset classes.

The fundamental principle of correlation (investment) strategy is to structure a portfolio to contain assets that are expected to generate high returns and combine low correlation assets – most of which will be generally highly volatile – in such a way as to produce a low-volatility portfolio.

THE EFFICIENT FRONTIER

Although it is beyond the scope of this book to examine this concept in the detail I believe it deserves to truly do it justice, it is worth noting here, at least in outline, the ultimate aim of correlation strategy: to identify and profit from the *efficient frontier*, being the ideal percentage mix of assets within a portfolio. A quick example should help to illustrate this strategy.

If we look at a portfolio consisting entirely of UK equities, we can identify that the high returns achieved over the last couple of decades have been achieved during a time of relatively high volatility. This is certainly to be expected due to the general relationship between risk and reward that we have already discussed.

If we next look at the performance over the same period of long-dated fixed-interest gilts, we can identify returns well above those produced by most other assets (except equities), but again with a high degree of volatility (only marginally lower, in fact, than the volatility of equities).

It might be expected that a combination of these two high-return high-volatility assets in a portfolio would have produced returns and volatility somewhere between the two individual asset returns. While this is true of the overall returns it is not true of volatility. Because these two assets have displayed between themselves, most recently at least, low correlation, the overall volatility of the portfolio will actually be lower than the individual volatility of either of them – the fundamental aim and concept behind correlation.

But, in what proportions should each of the two assets be held to maximize returns and/or minimize volatility?

The answer to this question is known as the *efficient frontier*. Identification of the efficient frontier is a partly scientific and partly subjective process, and in any event is based primarily on historical returns rather than likely future returns, though arguably the former is a guide to the latter. What the efficient frontier denotes, however, is the combination of assets (the *frontier*) that gives the optimum combination of low volatility and high returns. Stray beyond this frontier (i.e. combine the assets in proportions beyond those indicated), the strategy dictates, and the investor will suffer lower returns and higher volatility – clearly an unfavourable result!

Efficient frontier strategy is complex, but worthwhile studying for those seeking a more detailed scientific approach to portfolio planning than this book can hope to achieve, but be aware that it can only ever be one of a number of indicators of an appropriate balance of assets within a portfolio. We shall outline the efficient frontier as we progress through the asset class chapters, where we look at the correlation between these classes.

VOLATILITY, DIVERSIFICATION, CORRELATION STRATEGY AND THE EFFICIENT FRONTIER: A SUMMARY

The author acknowledges, as should the reader, that the strategies outlined above represent only a small cross section, numerically at least, of portfolio planning strategies propounded by a large number of (at least 'so-called") investment specialists. These strategies range from the ultra-scientific (requiring tremendous mathematical ability, but little common sense) to the neo-bizarre (many resembling horse-racing gambling systems).

The strategies outlined and discussed in this chapter are among the most widely recognized, respected and tested strategies in portfolio planning, but they can form only a part of any overall attempt at formulating appropriate portfolios for individual investor profiles.

Throughout the remainder of this book we look at many other aspects of portfolio planning, but we also regularly return to the strategies contained in this chapter and apply them to combining asset classes and investment vehicles within ideal investment portfolios.

4 Deposit-based Investments ('Cash')

INTRODUCTION

Deposit-based investments are those types of investment where, in return for providing an institution with the use of the investor's capital, the investor receives interest payments added to the amount of capital or paid as income on a regular basis.

With some of these investments the capital is accessible – either immediately or following a period of notice – and with others it may not become available (at least, without penalties) until the end of a predetermined period.

Cash is a critical element of almost all personal portfolios, because the capital value is not at risk and the investor may enjoy immediate, or almost immediate, access and it will almost invariably form the mainstay of an investor's emergency fund.

The main providers are the banks, building societies, and National Savings.

TAXATION CONSIDERATIONS

In considering these types of investment, non-taxpayers will generally be looking for accounts that pay interest *gross*. This then means that they do not have to concern themselves with having to claim back the tax deducted at source when they complete their tax return, or having to complete appropriate forms that enable them to be paid interest gross.

Conversely, higher-rate taxpayers will not be concerned with the gross rate of return; they will (or, certainly, *should*) compare the equivalent net rates of return from the various alternatives. As a quick and simplified example, let us take a deposit-based account that declares a gross rate of interest of 6% per annum. The non-taxpayer would receive 6% per annum, of course. The basic-rate taxpayer who, let us say, pays tax at 20% on this type of income (this tax position will be clarified later in this chapter) will receive a net rate of 4.8% (i.e. 80% of 6%). The higher-rate taxpayer, paying tax at 40% on the gross rate will receive a net rate of only 3.6% (i.e. 60% of 6%). If a competitor deposit-based account paid interest *tax free* (crucially, remembering the difference between gross returns and tax-free returns) at 4.5% we can make the following general observations:

- non-taxpayers should, without doubt, select the gross-paying account, receiving 6% instead of 4.5%;
- basic rate taxpayers are marginally better off with the gross-paying account (4.8% instead of 4.5%) but more care should be taken about comparing such other factors as period of notice and tiered rates for amounts of deposit;
- higher-rate taxpayers will probably prefer the tax-free account, receiving 4.5% instead of a net 3.6% (although, again, other factors must be taken into account)

As we discuss each of the main deposit-based alternatives we shall closely consider the tax implications for different categories of taxpayer including, in some instances, the individual's CGT position.

CASH DEPOSITS

The obvious type of investment that provides security of capital is cash – investments that are essentially cash deposits with an institution, and where the institution adds some interest. The best known of these institutions are the high street banks and building societies.

The investment return or interest may be fixed for a period of time or it may vary broadly in line with bank base rate. Generally speaking, a higher rate of interest is paid in respect of larger sums and also as a reward for long periods of notice. It is appropriate as an emergency fund element within an investor's overall portfolio because it is both low risk and accessible.

Tiered rates

The rate of interest payable on these types of accounts is structured in such as a way as to provide for higher rates to investors who:

- either opt for a requirement to give notice of withdrawal: the longer the notice period, the greater the rate payable.
- invest larger capital sums: the more that is invested, the higher the rate received.

Typical example: instant access account

This account offers, currently, 1% interest for deposit balances of up to £500. Balances of between £501 and £2,499 attract a 'premium rate' of 0.75% (thus 1.75%). Balances between £2,500 and £4,999 attract a premium rate of 1.75% (thus 2.75%). Higher rates continue on this tiered basis up to a premium of 3% over the small balance rate (thus 4% in total) for balances over £100,000

Typical example: notice accounts

For a given level of investment, an account requiring no notice of withdrawals (i.e. instant access) pays 2.5%. For a similar level of investment in the institution's 30-day notice account the rate is 0.4% higher and for the equivalent investment in a 90-day notice account the rate is 0.75% higher.

ADVANTAGES AND DISADVANTAGES OF DEPOSIT-BASED ACCOUNTS

Advantages

- the investor has immediate or almost immediate access to funds.
- there is no risk to the underlying capital.

Disadvantages

- there is no long-term protection against the effects of inflation.
- rates payable fluctuate in line with market interest rates and cannot be predicted with any degree of accuracy for the future.

HISTORICAL PERFORMANCE OF 'CASH'

It is often believed that deposit-based investments cannot and will not maintain their value in real terms, after allowing for the effects of inflation. History corrects this misconception, however. If we look at the rates of interest paid on 'cash' over the last three decades it is possible to identify that only between the years 1974 and 1977 was the rate of interest paid for money-market deposits lower than the level of inflation on a year-by-year basis: in every other year the rate of interest more than compensated for the effects of inflation and, over these three decades, the growth of money on deposit would have comfortably exceeded the required growth to compensate for inflation.

It has to be accepted, this being said, that I have in this respect used money-market interest rates that are by no means the rates payable to all or even most deposit-based accounts. These accounts typically pay rates far lower than money-market rates and thereby would not generally keep pace with inflation. However, read on: later in this chapter we shall be highlighting various cash-based investments that regularly *do* pay rates of interest comparable to, or even in excess of, money-market rates.

NATIONAL SAVINGS BANK ACCOUNTS

The National Savings Bank, which is guaranteed by the government, also provides instant access and notice-type accounts. Investments and withdrawals are made either through the Post Office network or can be effected by post.

Available through Post Offices (and through the post), National Savings Ordinary and Investment accounts credit interest on an annual basis, although this is calculated on balances on a daily basis.

Interest is paid gross, a feature that may be attractive to non-taxpayers who therefore do not have to complete declarations (as required on most other deposit-based investments) to receive interest in this way.

Ordinary account

This is an *instant access* account. It may be opened for a minimum balance of just £10 and the maximum amount that may be in the account is £10,000 per individual.

The first £70 of interest (£140 on a joint account) is free of liability to tax. At first this might seem to be a benefit but this account pays a notably low rate of interest which invariably 'loses' the investor more than the benefit of tax exemption. As an example, the rate of interest on the ordinary account , at the time of writing (late 1999), is 1.1 %, indicating a gross equivalent return to a higher-rate taxpayer of only 1.83 % (i.e. 1.83% less 40% tax = 1.1 %). The gross rate of interest on the National Savings Investment Account (see below), and indeed for most other deposit-based accounts offered by other institutions, is significantly higher than the Ordinary account.

The only real benefit to some savers could be the ease of accessibility of a local Post Office for deposits or withdrawals, particularly if there is no local bank or building society office or agency. For the purposes of portfolio planning, however, we must otherwise discount this option.

Investment account

This account is a one-month notice account, or loss of a month's interest where instant access is demanded. The minimum balance is just £20 and the maximum £100,000, whether the account is in single or joint names.

Rates of interest payable are tiered according to the balance of the account and these rates are usually competitive with comparable bank and building society savings accounts. This is particularly the case for (relatively) smaller balances, especially considering the required period of notice of only one month.

However, with many of the other accounts, there is often a facility to be able to make limited withdrawals without affecting the underlying interest rate structure. For example, the usual provision is that if the amount withdrawn without notice takes the account down to the next band level (of account balance), the interest that will be added will be based upon the lower tier level. Some accounts allow a maximum number of withdrawals each year, without notice, within certain limits.

All these considerations indicate that, when comparing different types of account, the various conditions – as well as the rates of interest payable –

need to be considered relative to the possible requirements of the investor.

THE MONEY MARKET

When an individual has a short-term cash flow problem, he or she must either seek to take advantage of, or arrange, an overdraft facility with the bank or alternatively acquire credit in some other way. Governments, banks, large companies and other organizations also experience similar cash flow problems from time to time but the amounts involved tend to be in millions of pounds rather than hundreds or thousands of pounds.

Money markets exist to enable those in *need* to have access to those in a *surplus* – for many millions of pounds of shorter-term borrowing facilities. The loans made are typically for 3- or 6-month periods, but can even be as short as 24 hours, or even overnight.

The *interbank deposit market* is the largest market for satisfying the need of banks to match their (generally short-term) income and outgoings.

LIBOR
The London Inter-Bank Offered Rate (LIBOR) is a fixed interbank rate that will prevail for any 24-hour period of dealing, and is determined at 11am each day, to provide a benchmark interest rate.

Large loans in the money markets are very often fixed in relation to LIBOR: for example, a rate might be determined as one quarter per cent above the variable LIBOR rate. Increasingly, loans to, and deposits from, the general public are offered at rates expressed as a percentage under or over LIBOR, although these generally appeal only to the more sophisticated members of the public.

MONEY MARKET ACCOUNTS

Quite simply, these are accounts that offer small investors access to money-market, or near money-market, rates of interest on balances much smaller than those previously required to gain the benefit of such high rates. Even very modest balances can now secure exceptionally competitive rates of interest.

Postal accounts offered (primarily) by high street banks and building societies

The initial development of high-interest, usually instant access, deposit accounts was postal or telephone dealing accounts, where a higher rate of interest was provided than those available through high street branches. These enhanced rates are sustainable primarily because of the savings in cost involved compared with transactions through a branch network, although occasionally there is also some element of 'buying in business': institutions offering very low profit margin (or even loss-making) rates to command a greater market share.

The investor should not need to concern himself or herself with the reason for the higher rates: after all, the investor should only be concerned with obtaining the highest rates available for his or her needs (taking into account accessibility, primarily).

TAXATION OF CASH DEPOSIT ACCOUNTS

Interest is taxable and income will usually be paid after deduction of 20% tax (exceptions include the National Savings Investment Account, which pays gross). Non-taxpayers can register to receive income gross or can otherwise reclaim tax deducted at source – usually through their tax returns. The income tax liability of lower- and basic-rate tax payers is met by the 20% deducted at source and higher-rate tax payers will be liable for a further 20% of the gross equivalent, after grossing up.

For interest from offshore accounts and National Savings Bank accounts, which are paid gross, lower- and basic-rate tax payers will be liable to 20% income tax, and higher-rate tax payers will be liable to 40% income tax.

MONEY MARKET FUNDS

These are pooled deposit accounts and unitized funds (unit trusts, OEICs and investment bonds, primarily) that invest on the money market through a spread of different interest-earning accounts and other securities. These may include certificates of deposit, bills of exchange and treasury bills, where the fund manager may seek to obtain advantage by adopting short-term trading positions in anticipation of trends in interest rates. Generally speaking, within a range of similar accounts, the higher the rate of interest being offered by a particular institution, the greater the potential inherent risk factor (once again, the risk/reward relationship).

Due to the pooling of money with thousands of others it becomes possible to obtain a higher rate of return than the individual could usually hope to secure individually, elsewhere. A cheque book withdrawal facility may be available.

The investor should, though, take note of the effect of charges either within the fund, or within the selected investment vehicle, or both. Consideration should be given to initial charges, annual fund management charges, and exit penalties on encashment.

Taxation treatment depends on the taxation treatment of the investment vehicle used, rather than following the normal deposit-based taxation rules.

TAX FAVOURED DEPOSIT-BASED ACCOUNTS

With existing Tax Exempt Special Savings Accounts (TESSAs) still capable of remaining in force, and Individual Savings Accounts (ISAs) open to new investors, it is important for investors to seriously consider these vehicles for deposit-based investments up to the maximum permitted contribution. Although these maxima are relatively very small, the rates of interest are usually very competitive. These are described in more depth in Chapter 15.

DEPOSIT-BASED INVESTMENTS: A SUMMARY

These are clearly an important part of an individual's financial planning strategy, first of all as an emergency fund, or as a pool of money from which regular investments to other asset classes can be made.

They are also a useful short-term home for the proceeds of sales of other investments, pending reinvestment. This 'home' could also be a safe port in a storm for part or all of the capital of an investor who is nervous of short-term prospects for more volatile investment opportunities.

Finally, cash can represent a legitimate low-volatile part of an investment portfolio in its own right, although the historical low returns indicate that an unduly high proportion of a portfolio in cash could lead to serious underperformance of the portfolio – especially in the medium and long term.

5 Fixed-Interest Investments

INTRODUCTION

In almost all cases fixed-interest investments are, technically, loans from the investor to the company or organization issuing the investment. They are usually known as fixed interest *bonds* (importantly, not to be confused with investment bonds issued by insurance companies) or fixed-interest *certificates*. They are usually issued with a nominal value of £100.

These investments pay, as the name indicates, a fixed level of interest every year (although some pay this amount in instalments each six months, or more regularly) from the date they are issued up to the date the loan is repaid, this date being known as the redemption date. In the meantime many are traded on the stock market at a price that can vary wildly, primarily depending on whether or not the interest rate offered by that particular bond is attractive against (then current) market rates.

THE RANGE OF FIXED-INTEREST INVESTMENT PROVIDERS

There are different types of fixed-interest investments, which can be broadly classified as below:

- National Savings
- Government bonds
- Local authority loan stock
- Corporate loan stock
- Permanent-interest-bearing shares (PIBS)

NATIONAL SAVINGS

The range of National Savings fixed-interest investments is described in Chapter 7, where we look at the National Savings regime generally.

FIXED-INTEREST GOVERNMENT BONDS ('GILTS')

Gilts: What they are

Trivia

Government Bonds are commonly known (including throughout this book) as 'gilts'. This dates from the time when holders of government bonds were issued with a certificate (evidence of ownership) which, although printed on ordinary paper, was edged in gold ('gilt-edged'). This 'nice touch' (as I have read other commentators describe it) was, in fact, to denote that all government bonds, being loans to the government, were backed by an equivalent value of gold held by the government as (at least in theory) further security of the value of the government's promise and ability to repay the loan at a future date.

These are loans to the government, issued with a nominal value of £100 – the price at which they will be repaid at a pre-specified point in time (with the exception of undated stock, which we will discuss shortly). The investor therefore knows exactly how much the capital will be worth at that redemption date: £100 multiplied by the number of bonds held. The investor also knows exactly how much income he or she will receive in the meantime.

How can the market price and yield be identified at a given point in time?

There are currently well over fifty government bonds on the market, each with different redemption dates and quoted interest rates.

Example - a fixed-interest government bond

One of these fixed-interest gilts has the title *Treasury 9% 2008*. The name 'Treasury' has no importance (other bonds are called 'Exchequer' or 'Funding' or 'Conversion' - similarly meaning nothing to the investor).

'9%' tells us the fixed yield granted to investors, this being 9% of the nominal value of £100. This yield is known as the *coupon* of that particular gilt, a title that should be contrasted with its *running yield* and its *redemption yield* (or *yield to redemption*) .Thus the investor or potential investor knows that, each year, he or she will receive £9 interest. As we are about to discuss, an investor who buys into this bond after its date of issue may have to pay considerably more, or considerably less, on the market than £100, but in any event knows he or she will receive £9 per annum interest for each £100 nominal value of bond (and does not, therefore, receive 9% of the value of the investment unless he or she coincidentally buys the bond on the market at exactly £100).

'2008' tells us the year in which the government is going to repay £100 to each bond holder. These may well not, of course, be the same people as those who originally subscribed to buy the bond at date of issue; many bonds will have changed hands many times since that date. The title of the bond does not tell us the exact *date* on which the bond will be redeemed, simply the year of that redemption. Further (simple) research would be needed to identify the exact date.

Some government bonds may be redeemed by the government not *on* a particular date, but *between two specified dates*. Treasury 13.5% 2004-2008 indicates that the government may redeem the bond at any time between (and including) the years 2004 and 2008. It also means, by the way (to confirm our earlier example), that holders receive £13.50 for each £100 nominal stock they hold.

What is the difference between the coupon, the running yield and the redemption yield of a government bond?

Coupon

As noted above, the coupon of a gilt is the yield the government pays on the £100 notional value of a gilt. This yield always appears in the title of the gilt, as in our earlier example of the Treasury 9% 2008. The running yield on this gilt was 9% from the date of issue and remains 9% until it is redeemed. An investor knows that he or she will receive £9 interest each year.

Running yield

Following its date of issue a gilt will be actively traded on the stock market and its price, as we have already discussed, will change according to market forces – primarily according to changes in market interest rates.

If the market price of the Treasury 9% 2008 at a given point in time is, say, £110, then a buyer at that time will, in effect, be achieving a fixed yield into the future of 8.18%, this being the effective rate of interest which £9 (annual interest payment) represents as a percentage of the £110 price paid. (Do not worry about the mathematical calculation, here: it is all done for you by the *Financial Times* and other quality newspapers).

This 'effective rate of interest' is more technically and correctly known as the *running yield* of the gilt at a particular point in time. It can be noted that the coupon of a gilt never changes but the running yield can (and will) change frequently.

Redemption yield

The buyer of the Treasury 9% 2008 at £110 (let us assume it is a man), is deluding himself if he believes that the true annual rate of return he will obtain in future years is 8.18%, the running yield. This is because he has paid on the market a greater price than the £100 redemption value of the gilt. You see, having paid £110 he knows – or should know – from the outset that if he holds his gilt until redemption he will receive only £100 – a capital loss of £10 per gilt. Even if he does not hold his gilt to its redemption date, but instead sells it in the market at an earlier date he should be aware that the market price will tend towards £100 the closer the gilt approaches redemption date. Thus all things being equal (primarily market interest rates) he should expect a continuous annual capital loss on the value of his holding against the annual income he will be receiving.

This loss can be expressed in annualized terms and deducted from the running yield to arrive at a 'true' consolidated annualized return – more technically known as the *redemption yield* or the *yield to redemption* (I will call it by the former name for the remainder of this book). The investor need not concern himself with the mathematics of the calculation of the redemption yield, these being widely available in almost all publications that list gilt prices.

Relative level of the coupon, running yield, and redemption yield
It is worthy of consideration that where an investor pays more than £100 for a fixed-interest gilt, the redemption yield will be lower than the running yield (as an annualized capital loss can be anticipated) which itself will be lower than the gilt's coupon. Where an investor pays *less than* £100 for a gilt the redemption yield will be higher than the running yield (because an annualized capital *gain* to redemption can be anticipated) which will itself be higher than its coupon.

Accrued right to interest under gilts

Interest on gilts is paid twice yearly, deemed in effect to be 'in arrears'. A seller of gilts between the two interest payment dates therefore misses out on a proportion of the interest since the last payment date, which will now be paid to the buyer at the next payment date. To overcome this inequity a seller of a gilt receives, as part of the consideration, an allowance for that earned-but-unpaid interest calculated on a daily basis. Thus if the next interest payment will be £1,000 and one quarter of the 6 month period (between payment dates) has passed, the selling price will be increased by £250. This is paid for, of course, by the buyer.

This mechanism avoids the distortion of gilt prices between interest payment dates because, otherwise, the price would tend to fall heavily just after an interest payment date (as little right to interest would have accrued) and rise steadily coming up to a payment date (because a buyer knows he or she will soon receive a large chunk of income on an investment not held for very long).

Categorization of gilts

Where gilt prices are listed, the range of bonds are usually listed under the following headings:

- 'short-dated bonds', being those with less than five years remaining to redemption;
- 'medium-dated bonds', with between five and fifteen years to redemption;
- 'long-dated bonds', with more than fifteen years to redemption; and
- 'undated bonds', which the government is not obliged ever to redeem, and probably will never do so.

To clarify this last category of gilts, the government is not committed to ever repaying the nominal £100 on these bonds. This should not be taken to mean, though, that an investor can never expect or hope for repayment of the capital; there are many ready buyers of these gilts on the open market. A few seconds thought will confirm why an undated gilt does not have a redemption yield (because there is no redemption date).

You should also note that long-dated bonds will one day become medium-dated bonds and, subsequently, short-dated bonds as the years pass and the redemption date becomes closer. This process has an impact on the progressive volatility, or otherwise, of its market price.

The differing volatility of prices between the different classes of gilts

The longer the redemption date on the gilt, the higher will be the impact on its market price of changes in interest rates.

Let us consider first of all an *undated* gilt with a coupon of 10%, trading on the market at a price of £100 and thus giving a running yield of 10%, which is in line with similar market interest rates available to investors. If market rates fall to 5%, this undated gilt will rise in price to £200 to continue to offer a competitive running yield of 5%. Thus a halving in market rates will lead to a doubling in the market price.

But will interest rate movements have the same effect on *dated* gilts?

No. Consider a very short-dated gilt, in fact one that is to be redeemed tomorrow, which also has a coupon of 10% and is traded on the market at a price of £100, giving a running (and for that matter redemption) yield of 10%. Now, if market interest rates should fall today from 10% to 5%, you should be able to see that the price of this very short-dated gilt will not change at all: it would be unthinkable to suggest that the price would rise to £200 when it is well known on the market that the gilt will be redeemed tomorrow at £100. In fact, the price of the gilt will not change because of the extreme proximity to its redemption date.

Expanding this principle, you should be able to imagine that the market price of a gilt with one week to redemption will also change only very marginally according to market rates, the price of a gilt with one month to redemption will be liable to change only marginally more, and so on.

It can therefore be confidently and correctly anticipated that undated gilts will be highly volatile in times of changing market interest rates, long-dated gilts somewhat less so, medium-dated gilts even less volatile and short-dated gilts not volatile at all – especially those with one year or less to redemption.

Taxation treatment of gilts - income

Income from gilts is taxable at the investor's highest marginal rate of income tax.

Gilts bought from the National Savings Stock Register (NSSR) pay interest gross, meaning that no tax is deducted at source but the investor must declare the interest on his or her tax return and pay tax on it accordingly.

Gilts bought on or after 6th April 1998 also pay interest gross. For gilts purchased before that date, however, gilts not bought through the NSSR will almost invariably pay interest net of tax (although with a residual liability for higher-rate taxpayers). For these gilts an existing investor can ask the Bank of England to pay interest gross – still meaning, of course, that the whole of the income payment is liable to income tax.

Taxation treatment of gilts - capital gains

Capital gains on holdings of gilts are completely free of liability to capital gains tax (CGT), although capital losses cannot be offset against an individual's other capital gains (as is usually the case, in computing liability, or potential liability, to CGT).

This means that gilts trading at a discount to their notional £100 value have additional attractions to investors who utilize all of their annual CGT exemption. At a time when the level of interest rates is historically low this will not usually be a great attraction because the vast majority of gilts are trading at a premium to their nominal value (i.e. their market price is higher than £100). But this tax consideration remains relevant to most undated gilts which, with a low coupon, have market prices lower than their nominal value: in these cases a fall in interest rates will (because they are undated, as explained above) have a significant upwards impact on prices, the gain being free of liability to tax.

Investment tip!
Higher-rate taxpayers who also use their annual CGT exemptions may be particularly attracted to low-coupon gilts for their greater exposure – tax free – to future falls in interest rates. Note, however, that they will still make a significant loss if interest rates rise!

Investment tip!
If an individual is attracted by the potential merits of investing in gilts it may be advantageous to invest *directly* into gilts rather than *indirectly*, through an investment vehicle, because investing through most

investment vehicles has the effect of turning the tax exemption on gains into a taxable liability. This is because it is the tax treatment of the investment vehicle that becomes the determining factor rather than the taxation treatment of the underlying investment.

Which type of gilt is appropriate for an investor?

With the wide variety of gilts available, short, medium, long, undated, index linked, how does one choose which is likely to be the most suitable for a particular investor?

The two main aspects to consider are the objectives of the investor, and his or her tax situation.

Objectives

If an investor considers a gilt to be a long-term investment that will be held until maturity, the decision as to which sort of gilt to buy will be different from that of the investor who sees gilts as a trading vehicle where gilts will be bought and sold as interest rates move.

If an investor intends to hold a gilt until maturity, he or she simply needs to decide the preferred term of investment and select a gilt with an appropriate redemption date.

Taxation considerations

We have already identified the attractions of gilts with low running yields and high capital growth prospects for higher-rate taxpayers in particular, with non-taxpayers generally preferring high-yielding gilts.

Consideration should be given, though, to investing in gilts through a tax-exempt Individual Savings Account (ISA), as discussed in Chapter 15.

Advantages and disadvantages of fixed-interest gilts

The main advantages of gilts may be summarized as follows:

- they are backed by the UK Government;
- the interest payable is secure and fixed;
- they may be useful for providing a capital sum for a future financial commitment, especially if the size and timing of the commitment are known;
- they are easily marketable if wishing to sell before redemption;
- dealing costs are very low
- low volatility, for shorter-dated gilts

The main disadvantages include:

- if inflation rates rise the value will tend to fall (fixed-interest investments will be less attractive unless the rate exceeds the level of inflation);
- unless purchased through the Post Office, the buying and selling costs of small holdings can be relatively high;
- potentially highly volatile – especially for longer-dated gilts;
- if market interest rates rise, the coupon under the gilt can become unattractive and disposal of the gilt then runs risk of capital loss.

Historical performance of gilts

Over the last couple of decades total returns from fixed interest gilts have been extremely competitive, although not as great as equity returns. These profits have been entirely due to a combination of high interest yields in the early part of this period but falling interest rates in the second half of that period – leading (as noted above) to significant capital gains in longer-dated gilts.

Interest rates have continued to fall, or at least remain low, in the late 1990s and so gilt prices have remained high. Demand has been fuelled not only by even lower European rates on comparable investments, but also by large pension schemes whose need to satisfy certain regulatory funding requirements has led them (for reasons beyond the scope of this book) to direct an unduly high proportion of their fund to fixed-interest gilts. As we noted in Chapter 2, surplus demand can be answered only by increasing prices.

Whether or not these high returns will continue into the future will depend on the movement of interest rates, at home and abroad, and also future regulatory changes to the way in which large pension schemes are encouraged (though not directly or deliberately) to over-invest in these assets.

Correlation of gilts with cash deposits

If we continue to define 'cash' as short-term deposits, it may be understandable how returns from cash and from *very short-term* gilts are highly correlated: a gilt with, say, six months to redemption has much the same qualities as a six-month term cash deposit.

Comparing cash deposits with longer-term gilts indicates, as might be expected, a much lower correlation the further away the redemption date of the gilt. For correlation strategy purposes, therefore, taking into account only the two asset classes we have considered so far, a lower-risk portfolio should consist of a mix of cash (or very short-term gilts) and long-dated gilts.

LOCAL AUTHORITY BONDS

Comparison with government bonds

These are essentially loans made to local authorities for a fixed term with interest payable to the lender. It is generally assumed that the government would meet the bill if the local authority was unable to do so, but the government does not have any contractual liability to act as guarantor. In essence, therefore, they are loans to a local authority, in contrast to loans directly to the government (gilts).

There is a ready market for these investments, although perhaps not quite as liquid as the market in gilts, and it can invariably be noted that the redemption yield is higher than for gilts because of the perceived additional risk of lending to a local authority as opposed to lending to central government, and the slightly lower liquidity (especially noting the relatively low number of these issues).

Beyond these considerations there is little purpose in considering these investments further because they so closely resemble the properties and behaviour of gilts. The author asks that you do not take this brevity to indicate an opinion that these investments are less attractive than their central government counterparts.

However, one particular difference should be noted: local authority bonds do not benefit from CGT exemption on gains, thus making these relatively tax-unattractive where they are traded 'below par' (i.e. at a market price below the issue price of £100).

Corporate bonds

These are a form of fixed-interest security which are in many ways similar to gilts. However, here the loan is made to a company as opposed to the government (gilts) or a local authority. The additional risk (at least as generally perceived) with corporate bonds is that relating to the financial strength of the issuing company: it is generally agreed that a company is more likely than the government, or a local authority, to be unable to meet its interest or redemption obligations.

Interest payments under corporate bonds are, technically, a charge against profit and not an allocation of profit. This means that the holders of loan stock must receive their interest payments, providing the funds are available, and this must be done prior to the calculation of the profits from which any shareholders will receive a dividend. This is why loan stock is perceived to be lower risk than equities.

Corporate bonds have a fixed rate of interest and will therefore be subject to the same market risk factors as gilts, which are primarily interest rate changes and, to a lesser extent, inflation (because higher rates of inflation make fixed-interest investments generally less attractive). The vast majority of corporate bonds have a redemption date, at which time the original nominal amount of loan (almost invariably £100) will be repaid.

They are not equities, rather they are a higher-risk version of gilts. Like gilts they have a secondary market on the stock exchange, which enables investors to encash their holdings other than at the set redemption date.

Taxation

The taxation of the interest and capital gains arising from corporate bonds is the same as for gilts. However, to qualify for the Inland Revenue concession of being exempt from liability to CGT, corporate bonds must be denominated in sterling, offer a fixed rate of interest and not be capable of being converted into shares in the company.

Permanent interest-bearing securities (PIBS)

A permanent interest-bearing security (PIBS) is a security issued by a building society. Technically it is a share but more closely resembles a loan from the PIBS holder to the building society similar to the other fixed-interest securities issued by other organizations discussed earlier in this chapter. They are shares, not loans, and therefore do not form part of the society's loan capital. This is not only an important technical distinction for the society but also for the investor because his or her rights – to interest and return of the nominal capital – are lower as a shareholder than as a creditor.

It pays a fixed level of interest (usually half-yearly) and it is irredeemable: there is no date on or by which the issuing building society has to repay – similar to undated government bonds except that, as shares, these will not be redeemed until share capital is redeemed (usually on the winding up of the society) as opposed to undated gilts which may (but probably will not) be redeemed at any time at the discretion of the government.

They are listed and traded on the stock market and the market price of PIBS will be affected by the same factors as undated gilts, although with some allowance for market sentiment relating to the issuing building society at the time. If long-term market interest rates are rising, the price of PIBS will fall. The converse will occur if rates are falling, of course.

There is, of course, no guarantee that the interest on PIBS will actually be paid. Unpaid interest will not be carried forward as an entitlement in future years. Thus PIBS are said to be non-cumulative and any unpaid interest will simply be lost. For these reasons, and generally because of the perceived higher risk profile of PIBS against government bonds, the redemption yield on PIBS will invariably be higher than that of equivalent gilts.

Taxation
Interest is paid net of tax at 20%, with a further liability only to higher-rate taxpayers.

Gains are free of liability to CGT for individual investors, as for gilts.

Guaranteed investment bonds

Worthy of consideration by fixed-interest investors willing and able to commit themselves to a predetermined locked-in term are guaranteed investment bonds issued by insurance companies.

Only a small number of insurance companies offer these types of bond and so whether or not competitive rates are available at any given point in time relies to a large extent on the intermittent desire and ability of those companies to offer attractive rates.

Quite simply, a guaranteed rate of return is offered over a specified period of years (ranging from one year to ten years, although not all terms are continuously available), either paid as income or accumulated as capital growth within the bond.

Being investment bonds the life office fund is taxed internally with no further liability on the taxpayer unless he or she is a higher-rate taxpayer (see Chapter 14 for a more precise discussion of this tax position). Rates on these bonds are quoted after allowance for this internal tax and so can, in effect, be treated as net rates for non-taxpayers and basic-rate taxpayers, although non-taxpayers can usually find higher gross fixed rates elsewhere (government bonds etc.).

FIXED-INTEREST INVESTMENTS: A SUMMARY

Clearly, fixed-interest investments must form an integral part of many portfolios, even if for a relatively small proportion. Returns over the past couple of decades have been very competitive, although these are by no means guaranteed to continue (depending largely on the future trend in interest rates), but important points in favour of fixed-interest investments are the guaranteed nature of future income and redemption payments (subject to the issuing organization not suffering financial failure) and the generally low correlation with many other asset classes.

6 Index-Linked Investments

INTRODUCTION

In Chapter 5 we looked at the various types of fixed-interest investments available, apart from National Savings. One of the disadvantages of such investments is that they do not specifically provide protection against the effects of inflation. If the interest rate paid on fixed-interest investments turns out to be higher than the rate of price inflation, the investor will have enjoyed what is known as a *real rate of return* but, conversely, if the rate of inflation exceeds the fixed return on the investment, the investor, even though on the face of it enjoying a 'profit' has, in fact, made a loss in 'real terms'.

Some investors may therefore be attracted to part of their portfolio being directed to assets that offer returns directly linked to (and usually in excess of) the rate of price inflation. These investments are usually termed *index-linked*. The 'link' to which the term alludes is the Retail Prices Index (RPI), measuring price inflation, and the returns offer protection against the impact of inflation either to the value of the investor's capital, or to the value of income produced from that capital, or both.

The range of index-linked investments is very limited, being:

- National Savings
- Index-linked gilts
- Other index-linked securities

National Savings investments are covered in Chapter 7 so in this chapter we shall look primarily, and importantly, at index-linked gilts with, then, a brief look at other index-linked securities, of which there are very few.

INDEX-LINKED GILTS

Index-linked gilts, as with ordinary gilts, are loans to the government with a notional initial unit value of £100 which the government promises to repay at a predetermined date in the future. The redemption value of the gilt will not, however, be only at the notional amount of £100 but will be at £100 plus the rise in price inflation from the date of issue to the date of redemption.

Example

The government issues an index-linked bond in the year 2000 with a 2% coupon and a redemption date during the year 2006. At maturity in the year 2006, it is found that the inflation from the date of issue of the bond has been 50%. The government will therefore pay, at redemption, £150 for every £100 notional bond.

The interest payable under an index-linked gilt also alters to reflect inflation. Therefore, the 2% coupon index linked gilt in its first year pays £2 for every £100 of notional value. If inflation during the first year averaged 5% then, in the second year, the interest payable would be increased by 5% of £2 to a total of £2.10.

It can be seen that index-linked gilts offer protection against inflation both on the investor's capital and on the investor's income (the coupon). Although the level of income on these investments is invariably small – the typical running yield is only around 3% – nonetheless it is protected against inflation and if the interest payment satisfies the investor's needs then he or she knows in advance that, in real terms, the interest will always satisfy his or her needs (unless, of course, the level of those needs increases in real terms).

THE QUOTED YIELDS ON INDEX-LINKED GILTS

Just as fixed-interest gilts have a coupon, running yield and redemption yield, so too do index-linked gilts.

Coupon

Typically the coupon on index-linked gilts is around 2%. However, it should be noted that this describes only the income payable on the gilt, in addition to which the investor's capital will increase in line with price inflation. Thus the true coupon on a gilt denoted as having a coupon of 2% is *2% plus RPI*.

Running yield

The nominal value of an index-linked gilt starts, as with fixed-interest gilts, at £100. However, this nominal value increases each year, for index-linked gilts, in line with increases in RPI, as we have already noted. The stated coupon is payable as a percentage of the increasing nominal value. However, the index-linked gilt will not always (and in fact will *rarely*) trade in the market at its nominal value: supply and demand will dictate its market price.

If the outlook for inflation is that the market expects it to remain low then the demand for index-linked gilts will also be low, putting downward pressure on prices unit the price is so low that the 'Coupon + RPI' yield becomes attractive. If the price of the gilt falls below its nominal value, the *running yield* will be higher than the coupon, by the same logic as applies to fixed interest gilts. Therefore an index-linked gilt with a coupon of, say, 2% trading at a price below its nominal value at that time will have a running yield of, perhaps, 2.5% + RPI (in any case, certainly higher than the 2% coupon). The converse applies, of course, if the market price is higher than the nominal value (which will tend to indicate that the market believes future higher levels of inflation): the running yield will fall below the coupon.

Redemption yield

Again applying the same principles as for fixed-interest gilts, if the running yield is higher than the coupon (meaning, as we note above, the market price is below the nominal value), a capital gain may be anticipated if held to redemption, when the market price must tend towards the nominal value which, of course, will be paid in full at redemption. This capital gain, added to the running yield, indicates a redemption yield higher than the running yield (of course) which itself is higher than the coupon. The reverse is true where the market price is higher than the nominal value of the gilt, as you should be able to identify.

TAXATION

The tax treatment of index-linked gilts is the same as for fixed-interest gilts.

Because the coupon on these investments is relatively very low and the potential for capital growth relatively high, these investments could, noting the exemption from CGT liability on the capital growth on gilts, be particularly attractive to higher-rate taxpayers – especially those using up their annual CGT allowance.

ADVANTAGES AND DISADVANTAGES OF INDEX-LINKED GILTS

The advantages of index-linked gilts are similar to those of ordinary gilts in that they are backed by the UK Government, the interest is secure and the amount payable is on a fixed basis. They can be used to plan for a specific commitment in the future, where it is known that the amount of that commitment might also rise with inflation from a present-day level, so it takes inflation out of the calculation on the basis that one cancels out the effect of the other. They are also easily marketable.

The added advantage of these gilts is the inflation protection provided, which means that any return calculated in respect of the present price to present redemption value will be worth the same no matter what inflation is in the intervening period and any interest being received maintains its purchasing power against the index.

The disadvantages are the same as for ordinary gilts apart from the fact that the disadvantage of no protection against inflation has been removed. However, the coupon rate is generally very much lower than under a fixed-interest gilt and this difference needs to be covered by either the increasing interest payable in future years and/or a greater redemption value, so as to provide for a larger overall redemption yield than would have been obtained under a fixed-interest certificate purchased at the same time.

If an investor wishes to hedge bets against inflation, he or she could, of course, choose to have a mix of fixed-interest and index-linked gilts.

HISTORICAL RETURNS ON INDEX-LINKED GILTS

Over the last couple of decades total returns from index-linked gilts have been poor, reflecting the progressively popular belief over this period that inflation would continue to fall and then remain low for an extended period. In times when the outlook for future inflation is low the demand for investments that are protected against the effects of inflation will also, naturally, be low. The principle of supply and demand therefore leads to the market price of those investments falling (or, at least, failing to rise significantly) to a level where supply matches demand. The volatility of these investments has also been low, reflecting the fact that prices of index-linked gilts are not generally driven by short-term influences; they are driven by the market's view of future long-term inflation which, of course, is unlikely to change on a day-to-day basis.

OTHER INDEX-LINKED INVESTMENTS

The options available are limited. An investor could choose to invest in either foreign government index-linked bonds which, broadly speaking, have the same features and behaviour as UK index-linked gilts.

However, various factors to take into account would be that if the expectations of inflation are high, which makes the return seem attractive compared to our lower rate of inflation, the currency might also be devaluing as well, which means that when the payment is reconverted back into sterling the return may be somewhat less than was obtainable under UK index-linked gilts.

Apart from these investments, a very small number of other institutions offer index-linked returns, the only example regularly quoted in the *Financial*

Times being an issue by the Nationwide Building Society.

CORRELATION WITH CASH AND FIXED-INTEREST INVESTMENTS

Index-linked gilts have a low correlation with deposit-based investments: the values of these investments are driven by completely different factors. They have a moderate correlation with fixed-interest investments, for the reason given in the summary below. With historically poor returns, however, and a continuing outlook of low inflation (at time of writing), the reduction in portfolio volatility by including index-linked gilts may be seen to be achieved by a reduction in the prospects for overall returns.

SUMMARY

You should be aware that, although the long-term inflation prospects are the key influence on index-linked gilt prices, interest rates also play a part. This can be demonstrated by the following example:

Example: influences on the price of index-linked gilts
At a particular point in time the redemption yield on a 10-year fixed-interest gilt is 6%. The redemption yield on a 10-year index-linked gilt is 4% meaning, of course, 4% + RPI. This indicates that the market believes inflation over the next 10 years will average 2% (making the two investments equal in value, as regards expected future returns). Now, if the market suddenly starts to believe inflation will average 5%, the price of the index-linked gilt must rise to a point where the redemption yield is only 1% (maintaining a 6% future expected return – equal to the fixed-interest gilt.
If, on the other hand, the redemption yield on the fixed-interest gilt rises to 8%, the yield on the index-linked gilt (6% in total) will look

poor. Demand will fall, driving down prices to the point where the redemption yield will be around 6% + RPI (8% in total).

You should take a little time to ensure you are comfortable with the implications of these demand drivers: in a nutshell, index-linked gilt prices will benefit where either the outlook for inflation is for it rise, or where long-term interest rates fall.

7 National Savings

INTRODUCTION

In this chapter we shall be looking at investments issued through the National Savings regime, and therefore guaranteed by the government.

We have already looked at the two deposit-based National Savings accounts (Investment account and Ordinary account) in Chapter 4, and now we shall look at the remaining National Savings investments, being:

- National Savings Certificates;
- Capital Bonds;
- Income Bonds;
- Pensioner's Bonds;
- Children's Bonus Bonds; and
- Premium Bonds.

In the absence of any statement to the contrary, through this chapter there are always minimum and maximum levels of investment. These vary from time to time and should be checked at the time of planning inclusion in a portfolio but, throughout this chapter, we note the limits at the time of writing.

NATIONAL SAVINGS CERTIFICATES

Period of investment and the nature of returns
National Savings Certificates are offered with a fixed period of either 2 or 5 years

At the end of the Certificate period, of 2 or 5 years (depending upon the term selected), the investor is offered an option to extend the certificate: a variable rate of interest is added and the investor is then able to encash the matured certificate at any time.

It is possible to withdraw from the investment during the chosen term but then penalties are imposed to the published rate which make the return on the early-encashed Certificate unattractive. In particular it should be noted that no interest is payable if the Certificates are encashed within the first year. In considering these investments the investor needs to be very certain that the capital can be tied up for the chosen period.

These are capital (i.e. lump-sum) investments where the rate of return is guaranteed, at outset, for the lifetime of the Certificate.

This rate is changed from time to time, but the new rate (denoted by a new *issue* number) applies only to investments from that time.

These certificates offer either a fixed rate or one that offers growth at a fixed percentage over the rate of price inflation over the period of the Certificate.

The rate of return on the Certificate is added to the initial capital and cannot be taken as income. This feature therefore obviously excludes these investments from consideration for investors requiring income.

Taxation treatment

Returns are tax free, making them particularly attractive to higher-rate taxpayers, moderately attractive to basic-rate taxpayers, and usually unattractive to non-taxpayers who will generally be able to find higher gross rates elsewhere.

Comparisons

It is worthwhile comparing the National Savings Certificates which provide a fixed basis for return (whether over two or five years) with the nearest equivalent: fixed-interest gilts (as described in Chapter 6). There is no difference in the security of the investment, both being backed by the government. It may be worth the investor who is considering fixed-interest certificates to identify the equivalent redemption yield for a government bond with an appropriate redemption date, noting though the different tax treatments: the income from the government bond is taxable.

The nearest equivalent investment to index-linked National Savings Certificates is, of course, index-linked gilts (as discussed in Chapter 6) and a similar comparison of equivalent (i.e. taking account of the different taxation treatments) yields might profit the investor.

CAPITAL BONDS

Period of investments and the nature of returns

These are also five-year investments where interest accrues during the five-year period.

Unlike the Savings Certificates which have a maximum holding per issue, there is an *overall* maximum holding for all issues of Capital Bonds.

Interest rates for the five-year period are fixed at outset.

The interest accrued is relatively low in the first year and becomes progressively greater each year. When advertised, it is the averaged rate that is usually quoted, although the progression of interest rates will also usually be shown.

No interest is paid if the bond is encashed within the first year and penalties arise if encashed after that first year but before the end of the five-year term – both aspects being the same as for National Savings Certificates.

Taxation

Interest is added gross, and therefore taxable. Indeed, the interest declared gross each year must be shown on the investor's tax return, even though it has been accumulated within the bond. Tax is payable on an annual basis, meaning that it is payable before the investor actually receives the benefit! Because the interest is paid gross these Bonds may be particularly attractive to non-taxpayers, and to a lesser extent lower-rate and basic-rate taxpayers. Higher-rate taxpayers should be able to find higher net rates of return elsewhere.

Comparisons

There are no close alternatives, offering stepped fixed rates, but corporate bonds and fixed-interest gilts both offer taxable fixed returns, although not by way of accumulation within the investment. Some banks and building societies offer stepped rates over a five-year period but these will usually be variable. Thus these Capital Bonds are quite unique.

INCOME BONDS

Period of investment and the nature of returns
These provide a regular monthly income, with a variable interest rate.

There is no fixed term of investment, but the bond holder must give three months notice of withdrawals or lose three months' interest.

Taxation
Interest is paid gross, making these bonds potentially attractive to all taxpayers.

Comparisons
The closest equivalent to this type of investment (a variable rate of interest, and some notice of withdrawal) is, of course, a deposit-based account with a bank or building society. Rates of interest should be compared before investing but, typically, Income Bonds will have greater attractions for smaller balances.

Guaranteed income bonds from insurance companies (see Chapter 5) have similarities only in so far as they also produce a regular income. The main, and important, difference is in the guaranteed nature of the level of the insurance bond income in contrast to the variable income from the National Savings version.

FIRST OPTION ACCOUNT

Period of investment and the nature of returns
A special type of account that has interest accrued each day at a rate that is fixed for the first 12 months following purchase. At the anniversary a rate for the following 12 months will then be advised.

There are penalties as regards interest being accumulated if withdrawals are made between anniversaries. If the capital is withdrawn prior to the first anniversary then no interest is paid, and on subsequent years the penalty for withdrawal between the anniversary dates is a 50% reduction in the rate of interest earned since the previous anniversary.

Taxation

Interest is deducted net of 20% tax, with no further liability for basic-rate taxpayers. Higher gross rates for non-taxpayers will usually be available elsewhere, but this account may have attractions for basic-rate and higher-rate taxpayers.

Comparisons

This is, in effect, a one-year renewable fixed-rate investment, with no close alternatives available elsewhere except by using a strategy of successive investments in, say, one-year gilts, fixed-interest term deposits, or one-year guaranteed insurance bonds.

PENSIONER'S BONDS

Period of investment and the nature of returns

This is a special type of Income Bond for a person aged 60 or over. It pays a guaranteed fixed rate of interest (in contrast to the Income Bond), payable for a fixed period of five years (again, in contrast to the Income Bond).

If withdrawal is made before the end of the five years there is a penalty equivalent to 60 days' of interest and the withdrawal in any case cannot take place without 60 days' notice unless the investor foregoes 90 days' loss of interest.

At the end of the initial five-year period the investor is offered a rate for the following five years.

Taxation

Interest is declared and paid gross.

Comparisons

These are very similar to the purchase of a five-year government bond and also to a five year guaranteed insurance bond (although in the latter case the low early withdrawal penalties of the Pensioners Bond provides an important difference).

The author suggests that these investments should be seriously considered by the over-60s who can 'have their cake and eat it' in so far as they are able to lock themselves into a fixed rate so long as that fixed rate appears attractive but if market interest rates rise they can take a low-penalty early withdrawal to find greener pastures elsewhere.

The nearest deposit equivalents from major deposit-taking institutions provide for a fixed rate of return for the agreed period, this rate often being (depending on the institution) set to increase each year the investment remains in the account.

CHILDREN'S BONUS BONDS

Period of returns and nature of investment
These are special bonds for children, designed to encourage parents, grandparents, or any other person over the age of 16 to invest on behalf of children on a long-term basis within a tax-sheltered environment.

The bonds are intended to be held until the child is 21. They provide a fixed return payable at the end of the first five years with extensions then being provided for subsequent five-year cycles, with a final maturity at the child's age 21. In addition to the interest accumulated during each five-year period there is a further bonus payment added at the expiry of the five-year period.

No interest is added if the bond is encashed within the first year. Thereafter penalties apply to encashments within the period.

Taxation
Interest and final bonus is added tax free.

Comparisons
All other five-year fixed-term, fixed-interest investments (including other National Savings products), although note the tax-free returns which frequently make them attractive, although with a low maximum investment (only £1,000 per issue at time of writing) their use is limited .

INDIVIDUAL SAVINGS ACCOUNT

This is a special, tax-free, immediate access postal savings account known as a Mini ISA. ISAs are discussed in Chapter 15.

PREMIUM BONDS

Term of investment and nature of returns

These bonds can be seen either as a form of gambling or as a legitimate investment, depending on your point of view and, more importantly, the amount of an individual's 'investment'. A statistic for the gamblers is that the odds of winning are 24,000 to 1 for each £1 invested. The equivalent statistic for investors is that the average annual percentage pay out is of the order of 3.5%.

There is no fixed term over which the bonds may be held and there are no penalties for encashment at any time.

Taxation

The tax-free returns may be mildly attractive, as an investment, to higher-rate taxpayers in particular, with a bit of a gambling instinct. Not really a serious or legitimate major part of an investment portfolio.

Comparisons

None, really, bearing in mind the 'might win, can't lose' nature of the 'investment'.

NATIONAL SAVINGS: A SUMMARY

National Savings investments should be considered as a part of almost every investor's portfolio, but it is particularly important to bear in mind the taxation position of the investor and even more important to make a comparison of the rates available at the time of the investment against its near alternatives.

8 Property

INTRODUCTION

In this chapter we shall be primarily considering investments in commercial property – that is, shop, warehouse, office, manufacturing premises and other commercial and industrial buildings. These are by far the most commonly-held types of investment property, but in recognition of the growing (although still, by comparison, very small) number of investors in residential property a short section at the end of this chapter looks at buy-to-let schemes.

Apart from the very largest investors and institutional investors it is usually not practical or possible for most people to invest directly in commercial property (except, perhaps through a pension scheme) and so this particular asset class – unlike all the other types of asset – can usually *only* be considered through collective investment vehicles such as unit trusts, OEICs, investment bonds and investment trusts.

THE NATURE OF INVESTMENT RETURNS

Investing in commercial property offers the potential for both income and capital growth: income in the form of rental payments from tenants and capital growth in the long-term expected increase in the underlying value of the property.

The risk to income is, firstly, that tenants may default on rent payments (usually only if they go bankrupt or into liquidation) or, more frequently, that it becomes impossible to find tenants for the property on commercial terms. With regard to this latter point it should be noted that certain types of property may be highly attractive to new tenants at a particular time but subsequently become unattractive. An example of this can be identified as office accommodation in the centre of certain cities in the UK: once highly sought after – and therefore attracting high rental yields – in a number of cities there has been a continued trend over the last decade for offices to be located on the edge of the city centre, or in purpose-built commercial parks or, indeed, in the suburbs.

If it becomes impossible to let the property not only does the income flow dry up but the investor's loss will almost certainly be compounded by a subsequent inability to sell the property at a profit if, indeed, it is possible to sell the property at all!

The risk to the investor's capital includes, therefore, the possibility of an inability to liquidate the asset at a reasonable price due to changing demand trends. More universally, however, there is also the risk – almost certainly a risk only over the short term – of falling commercial property values nationally.

HISTORICAL RETURNS

This risk – of falling commercial property values nationally – materializes very infrequently, although most readers of this book may remember vividly the commercial (and, indeed, residential) property crash of the early 1990s during which values fell some 20% over a three-year period – a loss that should be considered in the light of inflation during the same period of around 20%, indicating a real loss of around 40%.

This, though, was a blip (albeit a major blip) in the general trend for property values in the long term to increase at least in line with the increase in price inflation.

Historical rates of rental income have enjoyed very low volatility, fluctuating between around 6% and 8% – the upper range occurring in recent years and remaining high throughout the late 1990s, up to the time of writing (late 1999).

OUTLOOK FOR PROPERTY INVESTMENTS IN THE FUTURE

These high yields and low volatility make, in the view of many investment commentators, commercial property investment an interesting and (some would say) exciting prospect for the coming years. The yield of 8% is attractive, especially in anticipation that commercial property prices may be expected to rise, at least in the longer term, in line with inflation (or better). If inflation averages, say, 2%, the total returns from commercial property could realistically conceivably exceed 10%. This, compared to near alternatives (as we discuss below), is highly attractive.

Rental yields could fall, you might argue, but they can only really fall, in percentage yield terms, for one of two reasons: either rental income falls in cash terms or the value of commercial property rises.

Can rental yields fall in cash terms?

Most investment commercial property, professionally managed as part of a large fund or portfolio – is let, often to very large and financially secure tenants – on long-term leases (often nine years or more) with provision for periodic rent reviews (typically every three years), which may be stipulated to be 'upwards only'. In other words, rental income is secure for many years as long as the tenant survives financially and cannot fall below its current level. The author is aware of one commercial property fund, accessible to all investors, which holds property with an average unexpired lease term of twelve years, is 95% let (i.e. only 5% of the property remains vacant), with almost all tenants signed on upwards-only rent reviews. Surely this is attractive.

Rental yields falling due to increasing commercial property values

Given a rental income of, say, £100,000 per annum on a property worth £1 million, the rental yield is 10%. If the rental income remains the same but the property becomes valued at £2 million the rental income will fall. This provides a less attractive proposition for new investors but you should be able to quite clearly see that existing investors, although now enjoying a much reduced income, have made a 100% capital profit.

In summary, then, if one assumes that rental income in 'cash terms' is unlikely to fall on a good-quality, well-managed, commercial property portfolio the investor should be able to look forward to high returns for a considerable number of years into the future.

CORRELATION BETWEEN COMMERCIAL PROPERTY AND OTHER INVESTMENTS (MENTIONED SO FAR)

There is a minimal correlation between property and deposit-based investments: they are entirely different in nature. The only correlation relates to the income-producing feature of both investments though, even here, deposit-based investment returns fluctuate on a regular basis whereas property returns tend to fluctuate very little in the short and medium term.

There has historically been a strong correlation between property and fixed-interest gilts: both provide a regular and relatively secure income with, albeit in varying degrees, security of underlying capital. Until the mid-1990s the income yield on property has been consistently around 3% lower than the (redemption) yield on long-term fixed-interest gilts, reflecting the expected rise in underlying property (capital) values compared with no anticipated long-term increase in gilt values outside the redemption yield.

In recent years, however, we have experienced a *reverse yield gap*, with property rental income being higher than redemption yields on gilts by up to 4%. Add in to this the expected increase in long-term property prices and it can be seen that, at least in theory, property offers much better prospects than gilts during times of this reversal which has, apparently, been caused not least by a false excessive demand for gilts from pension scheme funds (as noted earlier in this book).

Overall, it may be expected that there will remain a strong correlation between property and long-term fixed-interest gilts, although with the acknowledgement that a correction in the yield gap may be due (leading to either a strong rise in property values or a fall in gilt prices, or both).

Property and index-linked investments are moderately correlated: if inflation rises the outlook for index-linked gilts starts to look more favourable, as does the prospect for capital growth in property prices (though not necessarily in *real terms*).

Property, therefore, the author strongly suggests, should be seriously considered as an integral part of many portfolios: good prospect for future returns with low correlation with the other asset classes held in the portfolio. We shall discuss the correlation between property and equities in the next chapter where we shall see there has also been low correlation between those two asset classes.

SUITABLE INVESTMENT VEHICLES FOR PROPERTY INVESTING

Unique among our consideration of asset classes it is clear that direct investment by most portfolios in commercial property is either unfeasible (portfolio too small) or undesirable (lack of diversification, lack of expertise in investment and management, etc.).

Thus where commercial property investment is considered appropriate the vast majority of portfolios will look towards a collective investment vehicle such as unit trusts, OEICs (both in Chapter 12), investment trusts (Chapter 13) or investment bonds (Chapter 14). Whichever of these is the most tax efficient for a particular portfolio depends on a number of factors, not least the relative taxation considerations of the vehicle and the investor, and these are discussed within each of the noted chapters.

RESIDENTIAL PROPERTY: BUY TO LET

I must own up to being something of a supporter of buy-to-let investments, in context, but only for those who accept the risks and rewards as part of a structured portfolio. Stories abound of landlords who make long-term 'fortunes' out of successfully managing residential property ('buy-to-let') portfolios, but one learns to question how many of these stories are true (although some quite categorically *are* true). Stories also abound of get-rich-quick speculators having their fingers burned.

Overall, then, this book will largely leave until another day or another author a detailed exposé of the buy-to-let market, contenting ourselves with a brief summary of the potential attractions and drawbacks of these investments within a structured portfolio.

DIFFERENT STRATEGIES IN BUY-TO-LET

The phrase 'buy-to-let' covers a multitude of strategies, ranging from the purchase of run-down terraced houses in run-down areas (generally let to appropriate tenants), through larger houses in areas popular with students divided into a number of single-occupier units (often termed 'multi-tenanted' properties), to small family accommodation in locations popular with such tenants (located near popular school, parks, shopping, etc.), and extending right up to very large properties suitable for rental to well-to-do families who do not expect to stay in a particular town or city long enough to make property purchase worthwhile.

Generally speaking, the higher the potential 'quick' rewards (which will almost invariably occur at the least salubrious end of the market) the greater the risk to those inexperienced in such matters. Tenants may default on payment of rent (oh, really?), wreak havoc with the house decoration, furniture, and even structure of the house, or generally cause severe nuisance to the landlord. The 'better the quality' tenants a landlord seeks to attract the lower will be the potential profit margins.

There are substantial dealing costs in this market, a requirement for close control and management (or payment to a third party to take over these responsibilities), and the prospect of potentially lengthy delays in realizing the underlying capital value.

Nonetheless, the opportunity to 'gear up' even modest amounts invested (by taking advantage of the availability of substantial borrowing facilities) can make this form of investment highly attractive, especially in the long term.

PROPERTY INVESTING: A SUMMARY

Although a purpose of this book was certainly not for the author to express personal preferences for different investment opportunities, for as long as commercial property prices remain stable and rental yields remain higher than long-dated gilt yields the outlook for property investments is surely healthy: either fixed-interest investments must fall in value or commercial property must increase in value, although perhaps not as spectacularly as happened in the late 1980s.

I therefore strongly suggest serious consideration of this investment for most portfolios.

9 Equities

INTRODUCTION

In previous chapters most of the asset classes discussed may generally be viewed as being low-volatile (except for fixed-interest gilts which have over the last couple of decades been quite highly volatile) and therefore suitable for the cautious investor, even without applying correlation strategy principles to planning a portfolio.

Equities, on the other hand, are generally (and usually correctly) perceived to be relatively highly volatile and not therefore generally suitable for investors with a low acceptance or tolerance to risk although, again, the author stresses that correlation strategy may make this generalization far too simplistic.

EQUITIES – FUNDAMENTALS

The term *equities* describes shares in companies.

There are a large number of different types of shares but, broadly speaking, for our purposes we can identify the main two types as being *ordinary shares* and *preference shares*. The vast majority of stock market shares, that are traded are ordinary shares, and it is generally this type of share that we mean when we talk about equity investment.

Shareholders are the owners of a company. The company can be either a public limited company (plc), with shares that can be offered to, and traded by, the general public, or a private limited company (usually denoted simply "limited" or "ltd.") whose shares cannot be offered to the general investing public.

There are many reasons why a company will offer shares to the public. Generally, it is because it wishes to raise finance for development or expansion and would prefer the option of offering shares rather than obtaining a loan.

Interest must be paid on a loan and the loan capital must be repaid at some stage. In contrast there is no requirement for a company to pay dividends on shares (the equivalent, in this respect, of interest on loans) nor must the capital ever be repaid.

Alternatively, shares may be made available to outside investors because the present owners of a private company wish to realize part or all of the value that has been built up in the company.

When shares are first issued by a company one of the factors that helps encourage investment is that the potential investor is not locked into holding the shares forever. There is a secondary market for shares (the stock market, of course), where existing shares are bought and sold.

By buying the ordinary shares of a company an investor becomes a part owner of that company. This means that the ongoing value of the share will be determined by the fortunes of the company – both current and anticipated – or, at least, by the perceived fortunes of the company (perceived, that is, by stock market investors generally).

If a company were to be wound up the ordinary shareholders would receive the proceeds of the assets on the break up of the company, but they are 'the last in the queue' and will therefore receive a payment only if anything remains after the other liabilities such as trade creditors and loan capital have been met. Usually there is nothing left after honouring these other liabilities and, indeed, a shortfall usually occurs, although the shareholders are not liable to make up this shortfall: they have a limited liability (the subscription price of each share), hence the title 'limited company'.

Preference shareholders generally receive a fixed dividend each year so long as the level of profits permits a payment to them, but in any event their dividend must be paid before the company can even consider making a dividend payment to the ordinary shareholders. Preference shareholders have a right to repayment of the nominal value of their shares in the event of the wind up of the company before a similar payment can be made to ordinary shareholders (although they rank behind the company's creditors in this respect, and in their claim to a dividend payment).

A person invests in shares despite the risk to potential loss of capital because he or she expects to obtain a rate of return superior to returns from less risky investments. In the next two sections we shall show how a shareholder expects to receive benefits in return for the investment.

HOW SHAREHOLDERS ARE REWARDED

The investment motivation for investment in shares is the hope and expectation of a flow of income return in the form of dividends and the prospect of a capital gain through an increase in the price of the share.

Flow of income: dividends

There are various factors that determine whether a shareholder receives a dividend. The predominant factor is that dividends can be paid only out of profits, after any contractual payments to creditors have been taken into account. The fact that there is a profit does not however mean that shareholders automatically receive or can expect payment of a dividend, and we comment more fully on this later.

If there *are* profits from which dividends *could* be paid, the next major factor is whether the shares held are ordinary or preference shares, and later we comment on the differences between these types of shareholding.

Capital growth

Once a company has issued shares, those shares will subsequently be traded on the stock market where the market forces of supply and demand determine the price. Obviously, investors who buy shares do so in the expectation that the price of the shares will increase. If market forces do not favour a particular share then the price of that share will fall and the investor faces a potential loss until such time as the share price exceeds the price initially paid.

In a later section in this chapter we shall be commenting on the factors that affect the share price.

Overall returns

Investors in shares clearly expect a return in excess of that available from lower-risk investments such as building society or bank deposits. This is a fundamental aspect of risk and reward. Historically the overall returns on shares have offered protection from inflation through investment in a real asset.

The investment return will, however, be a combination of dividend and capital growth and given that neither of these returns is fixed at any point in time, the return will be considerably more volatile in the short term.

FACTORS AFFECTING THE VALUE OF EQUITIES

It is crucial that investors or potential investors are aware that the market price of equities at any point in time is not solely (and sometimes not even remotely) dependent on the profitability of the company; the supply and demand for equities is driven by a large number of objective and subjective factors.

Interest rates
Equity prices may be influenced by factors common to the market as a whole, such as a change or anticipated change in market interest rates (highlighted particularly by the Bank of England base rate).

When interest rates rise the amount of profit used to service variable-rate loans, including overdrafts, will rise. This, obviously, reduces the level of profit attributable to shareholders. The greater the proportion of loans relative to the capital value of the company the greater the effect, and so companies with few or no borrowings will not be so adversely affected.

It should be remembered, conversely, that in times of falling interest rates the shares in highly-borrowed companies should prosper. Note that fixed-interest loans are not affected in this way.

Interest rate changes can also affect consumer spending because a rise in interest rates takes more money out of the pockets of those people with variable-rate borrowings (the majority, because overdrafts and most mortgages fall into this category). With less money to spend on other goods, demand is reduced and prices will be depressed, especially in times of prolonged high interest rates. Companies involved in the supply of consumer goods may therefore experience downward pressure on their share price in these circumstances. Falling interest rates could be expected to have the reverse effect, of course.

Currency fluctuations

These can have a significant effect on the profits, and therefore the share price, of companies involved in importing or exporting.

As an example, if a company imports raw materials as a first stage in a manufacturing process, the chance of being able to increase prices to its customers to absorb extra costs resulting from an adverse currency movement are seen to be limited and the market might expect its profits to fall. If, conversely, a company relies on export markets for a significant part of its profits, a currency movement that increases its selling costs (that is, a fall in the value of sterling) will have the potential of reducing its export sales (if the company imposes price increases) or reducing its profits (if it maintains its prices).

Political factors

Changing government fortunes can have an effect on share prices in general. As an example, if it is thought that a government is unpopular or has lost direction this will tend to cause a loss of confidence, especially among overseas investors, and cause prices to fall.

Company specific

Probably the most obvious of all the factors, yet as we can see by no means the only one, a company's share price will be influenced by factors that are very particular to that individual company such as, for example, a new product development which is expected to increase the profits of the company (most notably, over recent years, drug developments and the meteoric growth in mobile phones).

Diversification – a reminder

The risk to an investor's capital as a result of these different influences can be reduced by spreading investments. Even within the same industry an investor could choose to invest in different companies and extend the range by investing in companies that are not solely dependent upon that one industry. The risk can be further reduced by investing across a spread of industries or sectors. For the UK investor the risk of being totally dependent upon the UK economic and political factors can be reduced by having exposure to overseas markets. Finally, of course, the investor should consider diversification between asset classes.

HISTORICAL PERFORMANCE OF EQUITIES

Equities, over the last twenty years, have significantly outperformed all the other major asset classes in terms of total returns (income and capital growth). Unsurprisingly this outperformance has been accompanied by relatively high volatility which, however, is only very slightly greater than the volatility of log-dated fixed-interest gilts.

Although there has been high volatility of total returns, it is worth noting that the progression of dividend income over this period (and, indeed, over much longer periods) has deviated very little on a year-by-year basis from the long-term trend line. This trend has been consistently upwards until the last couple of years, when it has levelled out and now seems to show signs of falling, at least slightly – mostly due to the change in the taxation of dividend payments and the inability of pension schemes to reclaim tax deducted from those payments (both measures discouraging high dividend payments).

EQUITY SECTORS WITHIN THE UK – BY NATURE OF THE TRADING ACTIVITIES

We have briefly commented above how, by spreading investments among companies within the same industry, an investor can seek to reduce the risk to an equity portfolio.

It is also possible to spread investments across different industries. To enable investors to make comparisons between the performance of different industries, *Financial Times* indices classify shares into sectors, shown on the back page of that publication under the heading 'FTSE Actuaries Indices'.

A quick look at these indices can be instructive: as we noted in Chapter 3, significant differences in the performance of individual sectors within the UK can be identified. Moreover, the level of dividend payments also varies between certain sectors, most notably companies in sectors requiring high levels of capital investment usually pay (as one might expect) lower dividends.

If a particular sector has been performing well it does not mean that all companies in that sector have prospered equally. The index shows the combined performance of all the companies in that sector, some of which will have performed well; others badly.

Example

If we take the mining sector for the year to the end of 1999, share prices in the sector as a whole performed very well but shares in a company called RJB Mining performed badly. Of course, the performance of RJB shares formed a part of the performance of the mining index as a whole, meaning that the other shares in the sector must have, in total, outperformed the mining index.

EQUITY SECTORS WITHIN THE UK – BY CAPITALIZATION

The capitalization of a company is the total value of all the stocks and shares within that company at a given point in time, calculated by multiplying the number of shares by the current market price of each share.

The FTSE Actuaries listings on the back page of the *Financial Times* not only give indices according to the different trading sectors of companies, as discussed above, but also according to the size of companies by their capitalization. Very often it can be noted that, over a period of time, the shares in large companies have significantly outperformed their smaller counterparts, or vice versa. Indeed, quite frequently, over a period of, say, one year, large company shares may have shown significant gains with smaller company shares showing significant losses (or vice versa again, of course).

The oldest index is the FTSE 30 Share Index, which reflects the share price performance of the 30 largest companies by capitalization, but this is rarely quoted nowadays.

By far the most commonly quoted index, though, is the *Financial Times* Stock Exchange (FTSE)100 Share Index, commonly called the footsie. It is comprised of the 100 largest companies traded on the UK stock market.

There is also the FTSE 250 index which, as the name implies, is made up of the largest 250 companies traded on the UK stock exchange. The FTA All Share Index is actually made up of only 650 company shares – the largest 650 companies traded on the stock market.

At the opposite end of the (size) scale, the FTSE Small Cap Index is made up of a range of smaller companies' shares and there is the FTSE All-Small, the make-up of which is self-explanatory from the title.

By way of illustration of the diversity of price performance, at time of writing (January 2000) the respective performances of a selection of these indices, over the previous 12 months, has been:

FTSE 100	Up 5%
FTSE 250	Up 30%
FTSE Small Cap	Up 40%
FTSE All Small	Up 50%

You can easily see that the smaller the company, the much more likely its shares had been to rise in value, a result of a trend among institutional investors to see smaller company shares as being previously undervalued. Had we made the same comparison a year or so earlier, however, you would have noted that larger shares had increased in value by around 10% with smaller shares falling by some 20%: clearly neither category can continuously outperform the other.

GEOGRAPHICAL SPREAD OF EQUITIES

We commented earlier how an investor can reduce his or her risk of being completely dependent upon the fortunes of the UK economy by having exposure to overseas stock markets – probably, for most investors, through one of the collective investment vehicles described and discussed in later chapters of this book.

There is, however, in such diversification an additional risk – that of currency movements.

Example

If an individual invests £1,000 in French shares at a time when the exchange rate is 10 francs to the £sterling, the investment is 10,000 francs. If those shares increase in value by 25% the investment is then worth 12,500 francs. If, however, the franc has fallen in value so that there are now 13 francs to £sterling, the value of the investment in sterling terms is only £961.54 (12,500 divided by 13). In spite of the strong equity performance in local currency terms, therefore, the exchange rate has more than wiped out all gains when converted into £sterling.

Conversely, if the same strong French equity performance had been matched by a strengthening Franc (or Euro, to be a little more correct?), now 8 francs to £sterling, the holding would be worth £1,562 (12,500 divided by 8) – a rise of over 50% due slightly more to currency movements than to equity performance.

You should be able to imagine or calculate the effects where the foreign country's equities perform badly (against strong or weak currency trends).

Thus investing outside the UK carries the dual risks of equity performance and currency movements which can sometimes compound a gain or loss, or otherwise work against each other to moderate a gain or loss in £sterling terms.

TAXATION

Dividends

When a dividend is paid to a shareholder, the company must make a tax deduction from the dividend on behalf of the shareholder and pay it to the Inland Revenue as part of its total corporation tax liability. The rate of tax currently is such that for every £90 received by the shareholder by way of dividend, there is deemed to have been £10 paid to the Inland Revenue.

Although this represents a notional tax charge of 10%, basic-rate taxpayers have no further liability to income tax on the 'net' dividend received. A higher-rate taxpayer will incur an additional charge to income tax which grosses up the effective tax charge to 40%.

Capital appreciation in the value of shares up to the date of their disposal gives rise to a potential liability to capital gains tax. Depending upon the length of time for which the share had been held, there will be a reduction by way of taper relief on the amount assessable for tax. The subsequent rate of tax payable on the value of the gain after any taper relief has been applied to the profit made will then depend upon the investors marginal rate of income tax at the time the shares are sold.

CORRELATION OF EQUITIES WITH OTHER ASSET CLASSES

There is a low correlation between the performance of equities and that of cash deposits, index-linked gilts, and property. Historically there has been quite a high correlation between equities and fixed-interest gilts because of the market broadly maintaining prices at a level to produce a *yield gap*. This yield gap 'directed' (although by no means invariably was this direction followed) that the yield from gilts should be, say, 3% higher than the dividend yield from equities, the difference reflecting the prospect of long-term capital growth in equity prices.

In more recent years, however, equities and gilts have frequently shown very low correlation, reflecting an increasing market perception and strategy that the two asset classes may be invested in more as *alternatives* to each other more than being used in parallel: thus divestment of investments from one of the classes leads to increased investment in the other, with consequent price movements as the supply and demand situation changes.

Remember, though, the frequently low correlation within the equity asset class between different sectors, as discussed in some depth in Chapter 3, and earlier in this chapter.

EQUITY INVESTING: A SUMMARY

Overall, it is safe to conclude that equities have a low to medium correlation with most or all of the other major asset classes, and logic indicates this is likely to remain the case. This being so, diversification into equities (or, for that matter, out of them) as part of a portfolio should increase returns and reduce the volatility of a portfolio.

Reasonably consistent dividend yields (from a broad-based equity portfolio) and capital growth outperformance of other asset classes in the longer term must make equities an integral part of almost all properly structured portfolios. The use of correlation strategy can even make at least a small holding in equities profitable with little or no increase in volatility.

10 With-Profit Investments

INTRODUCTION

In some respects these are not asset classes as such; they are a combination of the asset classes we have already discussed. We have included them in this second part of the book, though, because they conveniently allow us to illustrate not only an important investment option (i.e. to have a portfolio managed, albeit indirectly, as part of a much larger investment portfolio) but also to conclude our look at classes of assets in the light of the diversification, correlation and efficient frontier theories and strategies discussed in Chapter 3.

A with-profits fund will typically invest in a range of investments. Most fund managers will invest more than 50% of these funds in equities – UK and overseas – with the remainder being directed to varying proportions in fixed-interest, property, and cash. In this respect it may be interesting and informative to note that fund managers thereby use correlation strategy (even though some do not use this exact terminology) to seek high levels of investment return with a low overall risk and volatility profile to the fund.

WITH PROFITS – THE FUNDAMENTAL CONCEPT

An investor who holds a with-profits type of investment – invariably with a life assurance company – is entitled to a share of the profits of the life fund. This share is distributed among with-profits investors through the periodic addition of bonuses.

Investments into with-profits may be made on the basis of a regular commitment (usually monthly or annually), this being the traditional type of savings/endowment policy, or (a more recent facility) by means of a lump-sum investment.

With-profits investments may be made either into a traditional with-profits fund or into a unitized with-profits fund – the latter being a more recent innovation.

A traditional with-profits fund accepts investments from a huge number of individual investors and the combined fund is then actively managed by professional fund managers with the (obvious) intent of making as great a profit as possible, although usually with a restricted risk profile. The profits made are then distributed to policyholders although the calculation of the level of bonuses and the charges levied by the life office for the administration and management of the fund are not openly declared to investors; they are said to be *implicit* charges and calculations.

Unitized with-profits are unit-linked investments. Again, the fund accepts investments from a huge number of individuals and manages the combined portfolio. However, the ongoing valuation of the assets held within the fund and the charges levied by the insurance company managing the fund are, in contrast to traditional with-profits funds, *explicit* – that is, they are openly declared.

This is not to express an opinion as to which of these two main types of with-profits fund may prove beneficial over the other; we merely (though importantly) note the technical difference between the two alternatives before looking at the practical implications of the differences.

TYPES OF WITH-PROFITS BONUSES

The bonuses added to with-profits investments are usually termed:

- reversionary bonus; and
- terminal bonus.

Different insurance companies use alternative terminology with, commonly, reversionary bonuses being called *annual bonuses* (reflecting, obviously, the fact that they are added annually to the investment) and terminal bonuses being known as *final bonuses*, reflecting the fact that they are usually added only at the end of the investment term.

Reversionary bonus and the reserve

Each year the insurance company assesses the profits made within the with profits fund which may be distributed to its with-profit policyholders. Some or all of this profit is then distributed to those policyholders as a percentage of the guaranteed sum assured (called the basic sum assured) under each contract.

Most reversionary bonuses are now declared and paid on a compound basis, meaning that bonuses are both declared and paid not only on the basic sum assured of each contract, but also on the level of reversionary bonuses that have previously been added to the contract. This means that the longer a with-profit policy or investment is in force the greater will be the effect of the bonus declaration.

Where the profits of the life fund in a particular year have been much higher than might be expected as a long-term average, most usually because of particularly good equity performance, the insurance company will typically withhold some of these 'windfall' profits in a with-profits fund *reserve*. In a future year when profits prove worse than expected, that insurance company may nevertheless then be able to maintain its level of payment of reversionary bonuses by subsidizing the bonus rate by transfers out of the reserve. In this way, the peaks and troughs of the investment world are, at least to some extent, smoothed over a period of time.

However, an insurance company's reserves cannot last indefinitely to mask poor performance on the investment side. Furthermore, if a company is adding reversionary bonuses at a rate higher than its 'current' rate of surplus earnings by drawing on accumulated reserves, unless investment returns or other sources of profit increase, there will come a point where bonus rates have to be reduced from those previously being announced. This has been the case over the last few years during which time, not least because of falling interest and inflation rates, investment returns have fallen below those enjoyed previously.

Terminal bonuses

Whereas reversionary bonuses are historically (but now to a large extent theoretically) paid out of the *income* gains to a life fund (which may be fairly confidently expected to be payable more or less at the same level in future years), that fund might also expect to make profits through the increasing *capital* value of its underlying investments.

As an example, a life fund investing in commercial property would expect to receive rental income and could therefore pay such rental income out in reversionary bonuses because the level of income should be expected, at the very least, to remain constant in future (as we discussed in Chapter 8). In addition to this rental income, though, the underlying value of the property may be expected to increase over a longer period of time and it is this underlying gain in the value of the asset – whether or not realized by a sale of the asset – which could be considered more volatile and therefore form the basis of the terminal bonus declaration.

Similarly, dividends from stocks and shares would generally be used to pay reversionary bonuses, as would realized gains on sales of shareholdings, but the general increase in value of the fund's shareholding could be considered more appropriate to the basis of the terminal bonus.

Over the long term the *unrealized capital increase* in the underlying investments is much more volatile than the income stream on those investments, and most insurance companies are loath to use such capital growth to meet the cost of reversionary bonuses, because such capital growth can easily be reversed into capital losses – especially in the short to medium term.

Accordingly, it is the practice of most with-profit companies to pay *terminal* bonuses as well as *reversionary* bonuses. These terminal bonuses are typically paid from the (volatile) capital gains of its life fund and are usually paid only to policies maturing in a particular year, although some insurance companies make an allowance for terminal bonuses in paying surrender values.

If an insurance company has enjoyed particularly good capital appreciation in one year, then maturing policies in that year can expect a windfall substantial additional payment – in the form of terminal bonuses – on top of the reversionary bonuses. However, if the stock market, property market, and gilts have performed badly in a particular year, then maturing policies might expect relatively little or no terminal bonuses to be payable although, in practice, most life offices maintain relatively stable levels of terminal bonuses from year to year.

Depending upon the length of time a policy has been in force, the final addition of a terminal bonus can make a substantial difference to the amount paid out – for longer-term policies, say 25 years, it can even double the reversionary bonus payment.

REVERSIONARY AND TERMINAL BONUSES: EXAMPLE CALCULATION

As regards traditional with-profits policies (for a discussion of the more recent innovation of unitized with-profits, see below), the way in which reversionary and terminal bonuses are declared by insurance companies can frequently be confusing and (though not deliberately) misleading for investors seeking to compare rates of investment return.

Take the following example. The Honest Mutual Insurance Company has declared, for the current year, a compound reversionary bonus rate of 5%. John Smith last year commenced a with-profits endowment policy with a premium of £100 per month which has a basic sum assured of £10,000. He has paid exactly one years' worth of premiums. This year his policy will be credited with a reversionary bonus of 5% of £10,000 = £500, but what effective rate of investment return has he received, in this first year, on his investment to date?

It is tempting to say '5% return' because this is the declared rate of bonus. Yet this 5% is not calculated on his invested monies; it is expressed as a percentage of the basic sum assured, so this cannot be the correct percentage. It is tempting, then, to say 'around 40%' because this is the percentage return the £500 bonus addition represents to the premiums paid so far, but this is clearly too good to be true. Although reversionary bonuses, once added, cannot be taken away, this is true only where the policy is held to redemption, or on an earlier death claim. Encashments before this time lead to the insurance company offering a surrender value that bears no obvious relationship with the accumulated declared bonuses.

In fact, it is impossible to assess the effective rate of return on a traditional with-profits policy until the policy has matured or been surrendered. This is unfortunate when attempting comparisons with other investment media, but it is a fact the investor has to accept if he or she chooses to invest in traditional with-profits policies. This is not to decry such an investment; merely to bemoan the inability to make meaningful comparisons of investment returns.

ATTRACTIONS OF A WITH-PROFITS INVESTMENT

For the investor who likes he idea of *asset-linked* investment (in equities and property primarily) as compared to investments that are inherently linked to deposit rates of return, but seeks to avoid the inherent volatility of such investments, the with-profits concept may hold great attractions.

Because of the smoothing out of investment returns that a life office achieves by holding back in reserve some profits in very good years of return, to be able to use later, there is more of a gradual rise in the value of the investment over the years than from one that is directly linked to asset values.

If markets are rising fast the with-profits policyholder will almost certainly not (at least immediately) fully benefit (as some profits will almost certainly be transferred to the reserve), but when markets fall he or she will be shielded from the full effect of the downturn and, indeed, will almost certainly still see an increase in the value of the investment by the continued addition of reversionary bonuses – probably at least partly subsidized by a transfer out of the reserve fund.

UNITIZED WITH-PROFITS FUND

During the 1980s and 1990s, as investment returns started to fall, one of the problems insurance companies increasingly came to anticipate was the prospect that bonus rates might have to be reduced. As we have commented on above, with the conventional with-profits policy a reversionary bonus, once added, becomes a fixed liability to the with-profits fund and insurance companies will not therefore declare continuing high levels of such bonus without the certainty that they can be met in future years.

In contrast, for unit-linked policies (see Chapters 12 to 14) the insurance company's liability, apart from any guarantee on death benefit, is limited to the value of the underlying investments purchased up to that time by the policyholder. Therefore, on a regular savings policy, no liability exists in respect of investments that may or may not be purchased from future premiums.

99

It was realized by an increasing number of insurance companies that if the unit-linked concept could be applied to with-profits policies, this would have the effect of reducing the insurance company's liabilities while maintaining the concept and attractions of with-profits.

With the unitized with-profits fund the policyholder secures units within this special life fund of the insurance company. Each year the price of each of the with-profits units is increased by the addition of a reversionary bonus, which means that the price then applying cannot fall. For policies that mature or pay out on death the company will usually add an additional sum as a terminal bonus. Therefore, the concept of adding bonuses is similar to the conventional with-profits policy.

However, although the price of a with-profits unit cannot fall, in that once a reversionary bonus has been added it cannot be taken away, the value of a policyholder's *holding* can fall. One might say that these two statements are contradictory and it is this apparent contradiction that makes the unitized with-profits fund different from conventional with-profits. The majority of unitized with-profits policies permit the insurance company provider to impose a *market value adjuster* (MVA) to the value of a policy under certain circumstances. This is alternatively known as a *market level adjuster* (MLA).

Market value adjuster (MVA) for unitized with-profits investments

The insurance company may impose an MVA where an investor seeks to encash units in a unitized with-profits fund before a predetermined date such as maturity of an endowment policy or, say, on a five- or ten-year policy anniversary. This MVA reduces the value of each unit below the published value and is most likely to be imposed during times when investment markets are performing badly – in particular during times of a stock market 'crash'.

It is imposed to protect the fund from the adverse effects of a potentially large number of encashments at a time when all but the fund's strongest holdings may be difficult to liquidate for a reasonable value. Bearing in mind the range of funds usually available to an investor, quite apart from the unitized with-profit fund, if this adjuster was not in place a sophisticated policyholder, or one with a market-aware financial advisor, could switch from the with-profits fund following a severe stock market fall into, say, an equity fund to buy a large number of units within the new fund at a very low price. Then when the market recovered he or she could switch back into the with-profits fund and, because of the gain under the equity fund, obtain substantially more units in the slower growing with-profits fund than held before – effectively locking in the gain made from the more volatile fund. This would be at the detriment of those with-profit unit holders who had retained their units in the fund.

The MVA may not usually be imposed at a policy maturity or on the life assured's death.

WITH PROFITS: CORRELATION WITH OTHER ASSET CLASSES

This is a very convenient point to bring our look at correlation of asset classes to an end, because with-profit funds hold a combination of the other asset classes we have already discussed; it is not an asset class in its own right.

This being the case, one might expect the *investment returns* from a with-profit fund to mirror the combined investment returns of the assets held within the fund and, subject to the smoothing effect of the bonus system and the use of the with-profits reserve, this is true.

One might also expect the *volatility* of the with-profits fund to mirror the combined volatility of the underlying assets, but this is not true. First, such volatility as the insurance company experiences on the underlying assets will be substantially reduced for the investor by the operation of the bonus and reserve system, as discussed above. The investor therefore benefits from the combined investment returns with reduced volatility.

Moreover, it can be noted that with-profits funds typically hold, say, 60% of the fund in equities, 15% in fixed interest, 20% in property and 5% in cash. Within each asset class a large number of different securities will be held. This combination can itself be seen to take advantage of the principles of diversification, correlation strategy, and efficient frontier identification discussed in Chapter 3. Thus the insurance company will seek to reduce the volatility of investment returns *into* the with-profits fund and further reduce the volatility *out of* the fund by the bonus system.

In summary, the author strongly suggests that investment in with-profits of part of a portfolio should be seriously considered.

11 Summary of Asset Class Features

INTRODUCTION

Over the last seven chapters of this book we have described and discussed the technical features and practical applications of different classes of asset. The flow of each individual chapter has not been consistent with the flow of the other asset class chapters because of their fundamental differences, and so this chapter is designed as a short *aide-mémoire* of the main features of each asset class, in note form. For further discussion of any of the points briefly listed here, therefore, you should refer to the respective individual chapters.

To recap, the assets we have discussed are:

- deposit-based investments;
- fixed-interest investments;
- index-linked investments
- National Savings
- property; and
- equities

The aspects we shall be covering are:

- whether the asset produces income or growth;
- accessibility, with or without penalties;
- security of level of investment capital;
- certainty of future projected returns;
- overall risk and volatility

You should note that, unless otherwise stipulated, we are in this summary chapter considering *direct* investments in the respective asset classes. Consideration of similar aspects through the use of investment vehicles is contained in part three of this book.

INCOME OR GROWTH

Deposit-based investments
Either. Income may be distributed or accumulated.

Fixed-interest investments
Primarily income, but capital growth may occur if market interest rates fall.

Index-linked investments
Primarily growth, the capital value being increased in line with increases in RPI. Income is usually payable, but at a low level.

National Savings
Depends on the type of Certificate or Bond.

Property
Over the longer period, primarily income but with expectation of growth – at least (but perhaps not much higher) than the rate of increase in price inflation.

Equities
Typically low level of income (dividends) except for high-yielding shares, with the largest rewards anticipated to come from rising equity prices.

With-profits
Usually growth, but a variation on this theme – distribution funds – offer primarily income. Unitized with-profits funds permit encashment of units to resemble income, if desired.

ACCESSIBILITY, WITH OR WITHOUT PENALTIES

Deposit-based investments
Usually immediate access, or very short notice, without penalty.

Fixed-interest investments
Most are freely traded on the stock market, allowing immediate access without penalty.

Index-linked investments
Most are freely traded on the stock market, allowing immediate access without penalty.

National Savings
Although usually offering ready access to the capital, encashment within the stipulated term of most of these investments carries often severe penalties to the published rate of return. Often no interest added on encashments within the first year.

Property
As we would mostly anticipate property to be held within an investment vehicle, rather than by direct investment, we generally defer an answer here, except to note that direct property investment should not be undertaken by individual investors in the expectation of easy access to capital.

Equities
Easily and readily realizable without penalties.

With-profits
Depends on the insurance company, and whether investments form part of a long-term commitment (in which case access does not come without penalties) or have been made on a single investment basis (in which case access may be available with no, or low, penalties. Note, however, the market level adjuster, if applicable).

SECURITY OF CAPITAL VALUE

Deposit-based investments
Totally secure except, in very rare circumstances, for the possible default in the lending institution itself.

Fixed-interest investments
Capital value quite highly volatile because of fluctuating market rates of interest.

Index-linked investments
Capital value quite volatile (although not to the same extent as fixed-interest investments) depending on the market expectation of long-term levels of inflation.

National Savings
Absolutely secure. Can never fall.

Property
Reasonably low volatility in recent years, although the early 1990s saw a near collapse in values. Expected future volatility to remain low.

Equities
Relatively high. Affected not only by economic factors but also by individual company fortunes and general market sentiment.

With-profits
Depends on the insurance company provider, but usually totally secure. Note, however, the market level adjuster, if applicable.

CERTAINTY OF FUTURE PROJECTED RETURNS

Deposit-based investments
None. Future interest rates are unpredictable.

Fixed-interest investments
If existing investments held, future income is absolutely secure and certain, remaining the same as it is at date of purchase.

Index-linked investments
Depends on future levels of inflation.

105

National Savings
Depends on the type of Certificate or Bond, but typically certain or near certain at outset, this being one of the main attractions of National Savings for many investors.

Property
Low volatility of rental income on good-quality property portfolios. Highly predictable to remain at least at current levels.

Equities
Dividend yields are relatively low volatile. Income therefore relatively predictable and secure within good-quality shares and portfolios.

With-profits
Reasonably predictable in the short, and even the medium, term depending on the size of the insurance company's with-profits reserve.

OVERALL RISK AND VOLATILITY (INCOME AND CAPITAL)

Deposit-based investments
Low.

Fixed-interest investments
Medium or medium/high.

Index-linked investments
Low to medium.

National Savings
Low.

Property
(Arguably) low. At worse, medium.

Equities
Relatively high.

With-profits
(Arguably) low. At worse (depending on the insurance company philosophy) low/medium.

SUMMARY

I would like to once again stress that this very quick summary is meant only for quick reference purposes and not as a definitive statement of the features of a particular asset class.

12 Unit Trusts and Open-Ended Investment Companies (Oeics)

INTRODUCTION

Unit trusts are one of a range of investments known as collective investment schemes. A person can invest into a unit trust either with capital sums or by means of regular (usually monthly) payments. The investor effectively has his or her money pooled with that from thousands of other investors, with the total sums involved being invested and managed by a unit trust manager. The investor is thus buying a stake in a pooled investment vehicle. The pool will contain a range of different underlying investments within its portfolio. Thus a unit trust is a means of diversifying, or reducing risk.

Oeics are very similar investments to unit trusts. In the first part of this chapter we shall refer specifically to unit trusts; almost all of this discussion also applies to Oeics and so only at the end of this chapter will we draw distinctions between the two vehicles.

UNITS

The total investment pool is divided into equal segments with each segment of equal value. These segments are called units and all buying and selling of units is carried out through the unit trust manager. There is no secondary market.

The value of each unit is, quite simply, the value of the total fund divided by the number of units in issue at that time. The units are bought and sold from the unit trust manager at this price with an allowance for a bid/offer spread imposed by most fund management groups (see below). There is, therefore, no aspect of price influences caused by supply and demand. Where there is demand for more units to be purchased by investors than those being encashed, the managers simply create new units. Where more units are being encashed than being demanded, the managers simply cancel some units. There is, therefore, total elasticity of supply.

BID/OFFER SPREAD AND SINGLE PRICING

When investors wish to buy units in a unit trust, they buy them at a price called the *offer* price. When they wish to encash part or all of their holding they redeem them back to the unit trust manager at a price called the *bid* price.

There is a difference between the offer price and the lower bid price which is called the bid/offer spread, this difference representing a profit to the fund managers which is used to pay expenses (including, frequently, commission to an introducer) and profit. The bid and offer prices are directly based on the fundamental net asset value, also known as the NAV, of the portfolio, and this must be calculated at least daily. The offer price is based on the NAV plus dealing costs, plus the initial charge. The bid price is based on the NAV less dealing costs. Typically the difference between the bid and offer prices is around 6%.

An increasing number of unit trust managers now buy and sell units from and to investors at a single price, with no bid/offer spread. Nonetheless these organizations need to make a profit to cover their expenses (and make a profit) and so will levy charges in other ways – either an increased annual management charge, reduced allocation of units initially, or exit penalties. See below for a discussion of the nature of these charges.

ANNUAL MANAGEMENT CHARGE (AMC)

After the imposition of the bid/offer spread the unit trust management group will seek to cover ongoing costs (and profit targets) through the imposition of an annual management charge.

This annual management charge is levied, invariably as a percentage of the value of the fund, to meet ongoing costs such as trustee fees, audit costs, administration and investment management costs. The maximum level of AMC must be specified in the trust deed and unit holders must be given three months' notice of any increase to this maximum limit with any increase above the maximum to be approved by unit holders at an extraordinary meeting. Fees charged usually vary between 0.765% and 2% per annum, although for certain funds, particularly those designed simply to follow a particular equity index (most commonly the FTSE100), the fee can be because low as 0.5% or even less (because there is less scope or requirement for discretion or skill on the part of the fund manager).

CHARGES LEVIED ON UNIT TRUSTS

Apart from levying charges through the bid/offer spread and the AMC, a unit trust manager can impose charges in other ways: primarily though one or more of the following methods:

- reduced allocation of units;
- exit penalties.

REDUCED ALLOCATION OF UNITS

In a distinction that is little short of cosmetic some unit trust managers do not impose a bid/offer spread, but instead grant a reduced allocation of units at the time of the initial investment. Thus an investment of, say, £10,000 might buy (usually single-priced) units only to the value of £9,500. It should not take more than a few seconds thought to realize that this has as near as matters the same effect as a 5% bid/offer spread.

EXIT PENALTIES

A more recent development, as a way of unit trust managers levying charges, is the imposition of an exit penalty. Trusts operating this strategy typically impose neither a bid/offer spread nor a reduced allocation of units. Instead they levy their required charges through the AMC and impose a reduction in units in the event of a sale within a specified period. Thus, for example, the investor may be granted 100% allocation on a single-price basis but the encashment value of the units may be reduced as follows:

Encashment within	Reduction in units (exit penalty)
one year	5%
two years	4%
three years	3%
four years	2%
five years	1%
thereafter	nil

Thus the unit trust managers rely on the AMC to cover their costs and required profit margin, covering their position in the event that the individual's investment might not remain with the managers for a sufficient period of time to meet this target.

FORWARD AND HISTORIC PRICING

Nowadays most pricing is based on the system of forward pricing. The investor does not know the exact price of the deal at the time he or she gives the instruction to buy or to sell; the transaction will take place at the time of the next valuation. However, there are very strict rules regarding the mechanics of pricing and the price finally used is the most up-to-date, accurate and the fairest price to all unit holders.

Some trusts still operate on historic pricing, meaning that the price at which units are traded is that of the latest valuation, but these are becoming increasingly rare.

DIVERSIFICATION

Unit trusts are established on the principle of collective investment and diversification of risk. There are many different funds available from many different fund managers but, as an example of this diversification, an equity-based unit trust must have a minimum of 16 different holdings within the underlying portfolio. The majority have significantly more. The maximum percentage of the portfolio in the shares of one company is 10%. A maximum of four holdings may be held in this way, thus up to 40% of the portfolio could be in only four companies. All holdings in other shares must not exceed 5%, and so the balance of 60% must comprise of an absolute minimum of twelve different shares.

An additional rule prevents unit trusts from having too much control over any one company in which it invests. The stake of a unit trust must not exceed 10% of an individual company's voting rights. These rules are clearly intended to ensure that unit trusts deliver the expected diversification without unduly involving itself in the day-to-day management or strategy of any of the companies in which it invests.

In the case of gilt funds, there must be at least six different gilts in the underlying portfolio and no more than 30% of the portfolio can be held in any one issue.

This diversification, of course, occurs only within the remit of the particular fund's investment objectives which, as we discussed in Chapter 3, may not significantly reduce the risk or volatility profile of the holding. Thus an investor should not consider that the diversification within a single unit trust will satisfy his or her aim for high rewards with low volatility; a spread of unit holdings is desirable.

INVESTMENT OBJECTIVES

Every unit trust must state its specific investment objectives. This enables the investor, or potential investor, to understand exactly what he or she has bought into (or are about to buy into). There are sector groupings which have been developed through the trade body of Association of Unit Trusts and Investment Funds (AUTIF).

As an example, if the unit trust is denoted to be an *income fund*, then it must achieve an income yield of at least 110% of the usual yield for that sector: if the norm for UK equities was a yield of, say, 3% then an *income unit trust* must achieve a yield of at least 3.3%. Furthermore a fund must invest at least 80% of its assets in the sector it falls into. Thus if a fund states that it is a UK growth fund then at least 80% of its assets must be invested in UK equities.

TYPES OF UNIT TRUST

There are many types of unit trust available and an indication of the broad range is given below. Some trusts that produce income will have the income distributed automatically, but some will be known as accumulation trusts. Accumulations trusts reinvest income within the trust to enhance the growth of the fund. However, for taxation purposes, the investor is treated as though the income had actually been received.

Most of the fund names are self explanatory (e.g. UK equity, Japan equity, Corporate Bonds, etc). As a (very) general guide the risk profile of typical unit trust funds may be broadly categorized as follows:

Low risk
Cash or deposit-based funds
Short-dated fixed-interest funds
Property funds (although only over the last few years; previously higher risk)

113

Medium risk
Index-linked funds
Medium-dated fixed-interest funds
Mixed (managed) funds

High risk
Equity-based funds
(specific sectors may represent the highest risk profile)

FUND OF FUNDS

These are funds where the investment manager determines the mix of the underlying unit trusts within the fund of fund unit trust. A fund of fund unit trust must have a minimum of five underlying unit trusts. Clearly such an arrangement offers further diversification and requires less active management by the investor or the adviser. The charging structure has to be studied carefully because such arrangements can be expensive in terms of 'costs on top of costs': that is, charges to manage the *fund of funds* on top of the charges to manage the individual funds..

TAXATION WITHIN THE FUND

Taxation of gains
Providing the unit trust is an authorized unit trust there will be no capital gains tax liability on such internal gains. Instead, liability for tax on those gains is, in effect, passed on to the investor when he or she cashes in the unit trusts. This can be viewed to be favourable treatment for investors who do not use their annual CGT exemption, as we discuss below.

Taxation of income
The underlying rate of tax on income generated by the fund's investments is 20%, although against this income may be offset annual management charges.

However, UK dividends are received by the trust net of taxation (notionally at 10%) and dividends paid out of the trust, to unit holders, are paid in the same way. This becomes, especially if all dividends into the trust are paid out to the investor, a *transparent process*: the investor is no worse or better off than if he or she had invested in the fund's underlying shares directly.

TAXATION OF THE INVESTOR – INCOME

A unit trust has two main types of income distribution:
 – A *dividend* distribution, which is similar to a dividend paid by a UK company and
 – An *interest* distribution paid by a unit trust with more than 60% of its investments in interest-bearing securities such as gilts or bonds (termed *qualifying investments*).

Dividend distribution
Income from UK authorized unit trusts will be paid net of a tax credit of 10%. This tax will meet the liability of basic- and lower-rate taxpayers. Higher-rate taxpayers will be liable for a further 32.5%, which will mean that they have paid a total of 40% of the gross amount. Non-taxpayers are not able to reclaim the tax deducted at source and are therefore disadvantaged in this respect as compared to some other types of investment.

PEPs and ISAs (see Chapter 15) are able to reclaim the 10% for the five years from 6ᵗʰ April 1999.

Interest distributions
The tax credit on interest distributions is at a higher rate of 20%. This will meet the liabilities of lower- and basic-rate taxpayers. Higher-rate taxpayers will have a further 20% to pay. Non-taxpayers *will* be able to reclaim the 20% deducted at source.

To make payments by way of interest rather than dividends the market value of qualifying investments must exceed 60% of market value of all investments held.

Equalization

Many unit trusts pay income twice yearly. Where investors purchase units between these dates, it is highly probable that they will have purchased an amount of income which they will receive on their first distribution,. Equalization is the identification of the purchase of some accrued income similar, in fact, to the payment of accrued interest on purchase and sale of government bonds. The equalization amount is treated by the Inland Revenue as a return of the original capital. This has the effect of reducing the true income element of the first distribution, thus reducing the amount of income tax due.

It also reduces the base cost of the investor's capital purchase cost for CGT purposes. This reduction of the capital cost will have the effect of either increasing the gain or decreasing the loss when the units are finally sold back to the manager.

TAXATION OF THE INVESTOR – CAPITAL GROWTH

A liability to CGT arises on the unit holders when they encash their units. In calculating the taxable gain the investors will be able to apply the indexation and tapering reliefs as appropriate and they even then can offset these gains against their annual CGT exemption. Indexation allowance and tapering relief are not available in respect of units in a unit trust which has at least 90% invested in assets which are themselves free of CGT, for example, bank deposits, gilts, or building society shares.

The vast majority of investors come nowhere near to using their annual exemption on a regular basis and therefore this taxation treatment, coupled with the tax exemption on gains within the trust itself, can represent a valuable tax avoidance opportunity for investors, especially with unit trusts that generate most of their internal profits through capital growth, as opposed to income.

If CGT is payable the rate will be determined by the investor's marginal rate of income tax.

Note, of course, that unit trusts are able to be held within existing PEPs (subject to certain restrictions) and may be held within ISAs. These issues are discussed in Chapter 15.

OPEN-ENDED INVESTMENT COMPANIES (OEICS)

These are a relatively new form of collective investment scheme in the UK, although the OEIC structure has been used widely in Europe for many years. The introduction of OEICs into the UK was made in order to bring our funds into a format that is more familiar to European investors. Unit trusts are based on the principles of UK trust law unique to this country and, as a result, created a barrier to sales in Europe where investors expect to see a corporate structure.

An OEIC may be conveniently described as being a unit trust within the technical structure of a company, and are much closer in nature to unit trusts than to investment trusts. Indeed, where throughout this book we refer in passing to 'unit trusts', you may generally take this to include OEICs unless otherwise specified.

Shares not units
Although closer to the unit trust concept than an investment trust, investors hold *shares* in the OEIC (as with investment trust companies) as opposed to units (as with unit trusts) as evidence of their stake in the pooled investment.

Open-ended investment
In the same way as a unit trust, an OEIC is open-ended in that the size of the underlying fund and the number of shares in issue will vary according to whether there are more sales than redemptions or vice versa.

Directors not managers
OEICS have directors to carry out the same functions as the managers of a unit trust.

Depositary not trustee
The underlying assets of OEICs will be held by an independent depositary whose role is very similar to that of the trustee of a unit trust.

AGMs

An OEIC must hold an AGM for its shareholders (in the same way as any other company) at which the directors must present an annual report to the shareholders and auditors must be reappointed at each meeting.

Pricing

OEICs are subject to single, forward, pricing. This is similar to an increasing number of unit trusts, but different to investment trusts (where deals are done on the price at the time, and market makers quote different buying and selling prices: their *turn*). The costs of buying the share in terms of stamp duty, the manager's initial charge, broker's commission and fees are shown clearly and separately, as with investment trusts.

Types of OEIC investment

OEICs are able to offer a range of different types of share and are able to offer cheaper switching between different underlying sub-funds. For instance, it is possible to have shares quoted in different currencies.

Taxation

Mirrors that of unit trusts, for both the fund internally and for the investor.

UNIT TRUSTS AND OEICS: SUMMARY

These vehicles give the investor convenient access to wide diversification between asset classes, sectors, and individual securities with specialist fund management.

The charging structures imposed by different providers should be investigated by would-be investors, taking note of the initial bid/offer spread, annual management charge, and any exit charges (e.g. charges imposed when the unit trust holding is encashed, this usually only applying – where it does at all – on encashments within a set period of years from the date of purchase). Generally, unit trust purchases should not be considered as a short-term holding because of these charges and to the generally volatile nature of the underlying investments held by most trusts.

Overall, unit trusts and/or OEICs should be very seriously considered for inclusion in the vast majority of portfolios, whether to be held directly or through ISAs. There are very few practical differences between unit trusts and OEICs for most investors, although OEICs may offer a wider range of investment opportunities and more efficient opportunities for switching between sectors.

13 Investment Trusts

INTRODUCTION

An investment trust is a public limited company (plc) that uses its capital and retained profits to invest in the shares of other companies in order to obtain income and capital growth. As with a unit trust, the investor is buying a stake in a much larger pooled investment. Investment trusts therefore offer diversification and professional investment management.

An investment trust is, however, a company, the sole purpose of which is to invest a range of other investments (in contrast to a unit trust which is, of course, a trust).

Following the stock market crash in 1988, many advisers commented upon the apparent resistance of investment trusts to the falls that occurred and as such they were promoted as a possible more stable alternative to the more volatile unit trust. The reasons as to why the investment trust appeared to be less volatile was possibly because of the different ways in which an investment trust can raise capital and also because of the different route an investor has to take who wishes to encash his or her investment. It should be noted, however, that there is a contrary view: that investment trusts may be more volatile than unit trusts. We shall be returning to this issue later in the chapter.

INVESTOR AWARENESS

When unit trusts were launched they were allowed to advertise not only at launch but also subsequently and therefore could continually attract new money. Investment trusts, on the other hand, after an initial launch were not able to advertise in the same way and therefore became less well known to newer investors.

Investment trusts come under the same limitations regarding advertising as any other limited company – namely that no limited company in itself is allowed to advertise its shares for sale except by reference to Listing Particulars registered with the Registrar of Companies and complying with the FSA. In practice, they tend to appoint management groups to promote and manage their investments and these management groups can advertise their services and do so much more than they use to. Being a company that offers shares in the open market, investment trust shares are treated by stockbrokers as shares, to be advised upon in much the same way as other shares.

INVESTMENT TRUST CAPITAL

A unit trust is dependent upon investors to enable it to start operating, whereas an investment trust raises its initial capital through a combination of equity and loan-based capital. When an investment trust is first launched the cash from the initial subscriptions for shares goes into the company's bank account for onward investment.

Because an investment trust is a company it can raise capital through a variety of methods:

- issue further equity (share) capital;
- issue preference shares;
- issue debenture (loan) stock secured by a charge on its own assets;
- issue unsecured loan stock;
- make use of bank loans and overdrafts.

None of these capital-raising routes is open to unit trusts, a fact which supporters of investment trusts identify as being probably the main reason why an investment trust is able to 'recover' quickly when there is a stock market fall: it does not need to attract new money from investors to be able to take advantage of depressed prices but can instead raise capital through other means. By being able to buy when asset prices are depressed, it can gain a substantial boost in its underlying fund value when the market starts to recover. This is of course subject to markets rising at a rate sufficient to counteract the costs involved in raising the additional capital.

DISPOSAL OF SHARES

When the time comes for shareholders to sell their shares they must do so by finding someone else who is willing to buy them. Unlike a unit trust where, if a unit holder wants to encash units he or she simply redeems the units with the trust manager, a holder of investment trust shares trades the holding on the stock market.

COMPARISON OF VOLATILITY AGAINST UNIT TRUSTS

In a time of 'free fall' selling of equities, the unit trust investor simply sells the units back to the fund manager who has no choice but to redeem them. Being in a situation where he or she is forced to sell underlying assets at a time when very few people are wanting to buy, the unit trust manager may have to sell the most marketable holdings at a price that really does not reflect their true value, these being the investments that may well show the greatest gain when markets recover.

The investment trust manager is under no such pressure: the investor who wishes to dispose of shares does so at the price that another investor is willing to pay on the open market, and the fund strategy itself is unaffected.

Perhaps this can be seen as being advantageous to investment trust investors, yet there is a contrary view. Where an investment trust performance is poor not only will the value of each share fall, but so will market demand for the shares. The price of investment trust shares will be driven not only by the underlying value of the shares it holds but also by the interaction of the forces of supply and demand for its own shares: falling values in the underlying holdings could trigger a multiplied fall in the price of the investment trust shares themselves.

This feature must be seen, however, in light of the fact that, unlike unit trusts, investment trusts are *closed-end investments.*

CLOSED-ENDED INVESTMENTS

The action of a shareholder selling shares in an investment trust has no effect on the funds being managed within the investment trust in that no cash leaves the fund. All that has happened is that there has been a change of ownership of the shares. There is a specified number of shares in issue. Additional demand for the shares does not lead to new shares being created (as occurs with unit trusts) and excess sales of shares does not lead to a reduction in the number of shares. Surplus demand leads to an increased price in the investment trust shares and surplus sales lead to a fall in the share price – in both cases, almost regardless of the trend in the value of the underlying share holdings.

Moreover, investment trusts have a finite life span. They must be established on a basis such that they will be wound up at a specified future point in time. At that time the trust (which, we stress, is not a trust but a company) must liquidate its share holdings and distribute the proceeds to shareholders. The closer the investment trust comes to this liquidation date the nearer the investment trust share price must come to the underlying value of the shares held.

DISCOUNT AND PREMIUM TO NET ASSET VALUE (NAV)

Because the value of shares in an investment trust is determined by the forces of supply and demand on the stock market, there is no direct link to the fundamental net asset value of the underlying portfolio. This is another significant difference between investment trusts and unit trusts.

If the demand for a particular investment trust is relatively weak, it's likely that the shares in the investment trust will trade at a *discount* to their true net asset value, whereas strong demand for the shares could have the effect that the shares are trading at a *premium.*

Example: discount and premium to NAV
The total assets held by an investment trust amount to £120 million.

There are 120 million shares in issue, meaning that the NAV equals £1. The shares are trading at 80p. indicating a *discount* to NAV of 20%. If the shares had been trading at £1.10 they would be trading at a 10% *premium* to NAV.

The yield on an investment trust is the relationship between income and price paid for the income. Where the price paid for the share is below its true net asset value, a discount has the effect of enhancing the yield. A price discount would also benefit a shareholder in an investment trust when the trust is wound up.

At the time of writing the largest discounts to NAV on certain quoted investment trusts (excluding capital shares) was around 30% while the largest premiums (invariably on highly specialized trusts such as certain emerging markets and speculative UK trusts) were around 40%.

TYPES OF INVESTMENT TRUST

Investment trusts offer a very similar diversification to that of unit trusts in terms of their investment objectives. The variety of funds ranges from the very specific (for example, funds investing in a particular geographical area) to the general (simply, an equity investment trust, for example).

Further divisions, not a feature of unit trusts, should be noted, the most common of which are given below, although the investor may well come across, and take into consideration, an increasing range of other variations on these themes.

SPLIT CAPITAL TRUST

Some investment trusts have different classes of share, catering for different needs of potential investors. With split capital investment trusts the same pool of assets is used to meet differing investment needs. The life span of these trusts is frequently ten years. After this time the company will be wound up and the underlying assets distributed to the respective classes of share.

When an investment trust is wound up, the pecking order for repayment of different classes of share is normally as follows:

1. Preference shares (if any), including any zero-coupon preference and stepped preference shares.
2. Income shares.
3. Capital shares.

The preference shares in a company, including an investment trust company, have been discussed in Chapter 9 and so no further detail need be included here.

Income shares are entitled to all of the income from the underlying portfolio during the running of the company, while the capital shares receive no income. When the company is wound up (no later than the end of its predefined life) or at an earlier stipulated date for the winding up of these particular shares, the income shares are entitled, at best, to a nominal value and, once this is repaid, the capital shares are entitled to the balance of the capital base.

The exact nature of the capital entitlement of the income shares will vary between companies and therefore needs to be identified by an investor, for each share. The capital shares will tend to increase in value at a higher rate than the increase in the value of the underlying portfolio in a rising market, and vice versa in a falling market.

Capital shares tend to trade at a discount which narrows as the redemption date approaches. Income shares, on the other hand, tend to trade at a premium which diminishes as the redemption date approaches. The prices of income shares are normally fairly stable, whereas those of capital shares are much more volatile. By definition, income shares will lead to a potential income tax liability while capital shares have no income tax liability but will be assessed on the individual for CGT.

ZERO-DIVIDEND COUPON PREFERENCE SHARES

These shares pay no dividend. Instead the capital value of the share is projected to increase by a fixed amount each year. Such shares offer low-risk capital growth as opposed to income and are, therefore, particularly tax efficient for higher-rate tax payers who are not otherwise utilizing their CGT allowances.

The return, however, is not guaranteed, although most holders of the shares are entitled to priority repayment on winding up. The actual entitlements are unique to each individual company and need be studied in detail by potential investors.

Because no income arises these can be very suitable for parents wishing to give capital to young children as it overcomes the problem of dividend income being treated as that of the parents and enables use to be made of the child's independent CGT allowance.

GEARING

A major difference between investment trusts and unit trusts/OEICs is in relation to their ability to *gear up* investors' capital by making use of their ability to borrow money to finance more investments than the capital from their shareholders, on its own, permits. Unit trusts are unable to do this. A unit trust is permitted to borrow only to meet anticipated cash flow deficits, for example to meet dividend payments.

This borrowing results, of course, in the investment trust paying interest to the lenders (whether these are banks or holders of, say, corporate loan stock). If profit from the investments this borrowing finances does not match the costs of servicing the borrowing, the losses are attributed to the investment trust shareholders, thus probably reducing dividends and certainly having an adverse effect on the company's net asset value (NAV).

If, on the other hand, profit from those investments exceeds the borrowing costs (as the investment manager clearly expects, otherwise he or she would not gear the investments up in this way), the 'surplus profit' belongs to the shareholders, increasing dividend payment capability and the NAV.

If an investment trust is said to be *highly geared* it has a relatively high proportion of its capital matched by additional lending. Here, shareholders benefit by more than their initial stake when the value of the shareholdings increase, but they will also lose disproportionately more when it falls.

Example:
The Adventurous Investment Trust plc has share capital of £80 million and loan capital of £20m. Over a period of time the investment portfolio doubles in value, to £200m, even after paying interest on the loan capital.

In this example the underlying portfolio doubled from £100m to £200m. If the shareholders' stake of £80m, on its own, had doubled it would have increased to £160m. However, the effect of gearing is that it has increased to £180m – an increase of 125% – after deduction from the £200 million portfolio of the £20m loan capital.

If, however, the underlying portfolio had decreased in value the shareholders would be less happy. Supposing the portfolio had fallen in value from £100m to £50m. If the shareholders' capital had fallen in value by 50% they would now have assets worth £40 million attributable to them. However, with £20 million of loan capital they have only £30 million to their name (i.e. the £50 million value of the portfolio less the loan capital of £20 million).

This example clearly show that geared investment trusts are higher risk than those with less, or no, gearing. However, the classic risk/reward relationship comes into play, and such trusts will certainly provide an exaggerated positive return when the markets are increasing, though negative return in a falling market.

There can be expected to be similar effects on income yields under income trusts bearing in mind interest payable to lenders or preference shareholders is a liability to be met before dividends payable to ordinary shareholders.

RISK PROFILE OF INVESTMENT TRUSTS COMPARED TO UNIT TRUSTS REVIEWED

Investment trusts have a very similar appeal to potential investors as do unit trusts because they are both collective investment arrangements offering convenient and cost-effective diversification even for modest or low levels of investment.

However, investment trusts are usually seen as representing generally higher risk than unit trusts due primarily to two main factors:

a) the gearing of some investment trusts; and
b) the finite number of shares in investment trusts.

Both of these issues have been discussed earlier, but it is perhaps worth developing the implications of the finite number of shares in an investment trust company.

The price of shares in any company is determined by supply and demand, and investment trusts are no different. It is easy to calculate the net asset value of investment trust shares, being the value of the assets held by the company divided by the number of shares in issue (making allowance for certain factors, most importantly the gearing of the company).

However, excess demand (over supply) for shares in an investment trust will invariably lead to buyers demanding a higher price than they could previously have expected. This increased demand will usually have arisen as a result of good performance of the investment trust's assets, meaning not only that the investor will benefit from increased NAV but also, probably, from a premium over this performance as demand increases. Conversely, shares in poorly performing investment trusts are likely to suffer not only from a falling NAV but, as demand falls, an even greater fall in the share price may result.

The price of shares in investment trusts may, as a result, trade at a premium to NAV (meaning that the investor is paying more for each share than the value of assets held per share) or at a discount (meaning, in fact, that the investor is buying into the shares at a lower price than the value of assets held in respect of that share). Furthermore the level of premium or discount varies widely between investment trusts. As an example, on a particular (random) day around the time of writing the highest discount to NAV of an investment trust was 47.8% (Invesco Enterprise) and the highest premium 49.2% (Indonesia Enterprise).

Market sentiment can, and does, change over time and so these discounts and premiums can be highly volatile, as can the NAV, of course. This dual volatility, the author suggests, makes investment trusts generally more volatile than unit trusts. This is not a criticism, of course: many investors seek to use higher volatility to their advantage (as we outlined in Chapter 3, for example).

COSTS

Initial and exit costs

Stockbroker's commission is typically between 1% and 1.65%, both on acquiring and disposing of shares, subject to a minimum of, say, £25. Stamp duty on purchases is 0.5% of the investment and the 'turn' taken by the market maker (the difference between the prices at which he or she is prepared to buy and sell) is generally around 1.5%.

It is dangerous to be too generalistic, I suppose, but for an average sized investment the total initial and exit costs may amount typically to around 4% (although much smaller for larger purchases, especially where transacted through low-priced execution-only dealers). This may give an idea of the term over which the investment should be anticipated to be held before a true profit on the transaction can be enjoyed.

Annual cost

This will often be around 0.5% p.a. on the value of portfolio but for specialist or new trusts can be higher. Where a manager acts for a number of trusts and can spread the burden of administration and management costs among a number of trusts the costs may be a little lower. There is the same external regulation on costs that are applied to unit trusts, not least to prevent abuse of the fact that annual management charges are levied by investment trusts in not quite so transparent a way as for unit trusts.

TAXATION OF INVESTMENT TRUSTS – WITHIN THE FUND

Gains

Although an investment trust is a company, gains made by the fund on the sale of shares will not be liable to tax within that fund; instead, as noted below, the gain is passed on to the investor for assessment to CGT.

Income

Moreover, no further liability to corporation tax arises on dividends from UK companies. Again, as noted below, shareholders will themselves be assessed to income tax on dividends paid *by* (not *to)* the investment trust. Other income generated within the investment rust company is liable to corporation tax (e.g. interest on cash balances, and interest from gilts), but the company may set management fees against this liability.

The taxation treatment of the investment trust company fund is very close to the taxation treatment of a unit trust and an OEIC (see Chapter 12).

TAXATION OF INVESTMENT TRUSTS – THE INVESTOR

Dividend income

Because an investment trust company is a company, not a trust, dividends are considered to be share dividends just as with any other company. See Chapter 9 for a fuller description. PEPs and ISAs are able to reclaim the 10% for the five years from 6th April 1999 (see Chapter 15).

Capital growth

The investor is liable to CGT on gains on the sale of investment trusts, as with ordinary shares in any other company, subject of course to being able to apply indexation and tapering reliefs as appropriate and taking into account available CGT annual allowance.

CGT indexation allowance or tapering relief will not be available in respect of units in an investment trust that has at least 90% invested in assets that are themselves free of CGT, for example, bank deposits, gilts, or building society shares. This is to ensure that an investor does not obtain relief against CGT through an investment trust investment where there would have been no such relief for a direct investment into those areas.

ADVANTAGES AND DISADVANTAGES OF INVESTMENT TRUST INVESTMENT IN COMPARISON TO UNIT TRUSTS

These are generally the same as for unit trusts and OEICs (Chapter 12) although, as noted earlier, investment trusts are generally (and correctly, in the view of the author) perceived to be a higher-risk vehicle than those near alternatives.

Split capital trusts offer the investor an additional degree of focus on the level of risk and reward desired for this part of a portfolio. For instance, a non-taxpaying pensioner who needs income and is prepared to take a certain amount of risk to capital might favour an income share, whereas a higher-rate taxpayer not in need of income and wishing to avoid exposure to too much risk, might favour a zero-dividend preference share. A higher-rate tax payer prepared to take even more risk with capital might be attracted to capital shares.

For those investors who wish to invest in volatile or high-risk areas investment trusts arguably offer a potential advantage over unit trusts. We noted earlier that an investment trust does not have to realize investments when an investor seeks to liquidate the holding: the investment trust is unaffected because it simply has a different shareholder. This could be particularly relevant for highly volatile funds because in a falling market the manager of the investment trust can choose to hold on to stock judged to be undervalued whereas a unit trust manager may be forced to sell stock that ideally he or she would have wished to hold. There is therefore less likely to be the downward pressure in a falling market that can be increased by having to have investments sold to meet withdrawal requests. However, who can tell whether the 'fallen market' will not fall yet further?

Volatility within investment trusts, over and above the volatility of an equity portfolio generally, can be exaggerated by gearing of the loan capital, discounts to NAV widening and narrowing and the prior rights of other classes of share or capital (all as discussed above).

As regards the gearing of investment trusts, however, the investor should note that many investment trusts are very lowly geared or have no borrowings at all and, where this is the case, the gearing comparison between unit trusts and investment trusts in general is inappropriate.

The discount to NAV of most investment trusts is often seen as a potential advantage, but it is only advantageous if the discount narrows. The widening of a discount, quite apart from meaning that the share price falls well below the underlying NAV per share, could also lead to a problem in attracting new money into a fund by issuing additional shares: why should a potential investor buy into an investment trust company at the price that reflects the previous underperformance of investment management?

Historically, investment trusts were said to have lower initial investment costs, because they have no actual initial charges and to have lower annual management costs. The situation has changed through competitive forces in the marketplace and in general the charges of unit trusts have decreased and the charges of some recently launched investment trusts have shown an increase. So beware of generalizations and examine the specific charges of individual products, in particular taking into account not only the costs of buying and holding (annual management charge), but also the costs of selling (dealing and exit charges).

14 Investment Bonds

INTRODUCTION

Investment bonds are collective investments issued by life assurance companies that are, technically, single-premium life assurance policies

To a large extent they have the same purpose as other collective investments such as unit trusts and investment trusts in that they are aimed at investors who either want income or growth or a mix of both, with returns are linked to asset-based investments.

Because such bonds are issued primarily for investment and not life assurance, the life assurance element is very often no more than 100% of the fund value at any point in time although it might be slightly higher – typically 101% to establish an element of 'true' life assurance (i.e. 1% over the fund value). The inclusion of this death benefit ensures that these bonds qualify for the tax regime that applies to life assurance office funds.

The types of funds offered by investment bonds are very similar to those provided by unit and investment trusts: indeed, with some companies the underlying investments can be linked directly to unit trust funds.

The relative attraction, or otherwise, of investment bonds against unit trusts and investment trusts is almost totally dependant on the attraction or otherwise of each vehicle's tax regime for a particular investor.

UNITS

As with unit trusts, the total investment pool is divided into equal segments called units, and each unit is of equal value within the fund. The buying and selling of units is carried out through the life office even when units are being obtained for a particular unit trust fund.

SIMILARITIES BETWEEN INVESTMENT BONDS AND UNIT TRUSTS

There are a great many similarities between investment bonds and unit trusts. Therefore, rather than simply repeat the detail and discussion from Chapter 13 in these aspects, we merely list below the features both vehicles have in common:

- bid/offer spread and single pricing
- unit allocation
- annual management charges
- open-ended investment
- historic pricing
- range of investment funds

DIFFERENCES BETWEEN INVESTMENT BONDS AND UNIT TRUSTS

By far the main difference between these two investment vehicles relates to the taxation treatment on profits within the fund and on payments made out of the fund to unit holders. The specific taxation treatment of bonds is discussed in some detail below, as are the following other differences:

- no dividend payments are made from investment bonds;
- switches are allowed between funds without crystallizing a potential tax liability; and
- increments may be effected to investment bonds with potentially favourable tax implications.

TAXATION

Internal tax treatment of insurance bonds

When a policy qualifies as a UK authorized life assurance policy, the underlying tax treatment of the funds is different to that of unit trusts, OEICs and investment trusts. After deducting expenses, the net amount of investment income *and capital gains* (this latter aspect is where the difference lies, against the other collective investment vehicles discussed in earlier chapters) is subject to tax in respect of the policyholders' share of the profits, at 20%.

The expenses of acquiring new business can be spread over a period of seven years for the purposes of calculating this internal taxation liability. This, and other accounting and taxation considerations, can lead, some commentators suggest, to an effective rate of tax up to 3% lower than the notional rate of 20%.

Because life companies continually have money coming into these investment funds, both in the form of single investments and from regular savings plans, they are very often able to meet encashments of units from this 'new money', and are therefore able to defer realization of investment assets for a long period. This defers realization of the profit on those assets, thereby deferring tax liability on those gains. The benefit of this deferral may be claimed to enhance the underlying return being achieved on the fund.

Chargeable events

Before investigating further the taxation treatment of the investor (as opposed to the tax treatment of the fund), it is first of all necessary to understand the circumstances under which a liability to tax on the investor might arise. There is no further potential liability on the investor until a chargeable *event* occurs.

The following occurrences are chargeable events:

- death;

- maturity;
- surrender;
- certain part surrenders (see below);
- policy loan;
- assignment for money or moneys worth.

TAXATION LIABILITY ON THE INVESTOR

First of all it is important to note that any further liability to tax on the gains within an investment bond is a liability to income tax, not CGT as might be expected because the profit on an investment bond appears to be a capital gain.

Higher-rate taxpayers
If an investor is a higher-rate taxpayer when a chargeable event occurs, additional income tax is due on the gain within the bond, representing the difference between the higher rate of tax (40%) and the basic rate of tax deemed to have already been paid by the fund. With the basic rate of tax of 23%, for example, the additional tax charge will be 17%.

The partial withdrawal (5%) concession should particularly be noted, and is detailed below.

It is useful and important to note that the additional tax charge does not apply at the time the gain accrues; it is imposed only on the happening of a chargeable event. This can be particularly useful for investors who are higher-rate taxpayers because the gain accrues under the bond but falls into a lower tax band during the year of the chargeable event.

Other taxpayers
Generally speaking, there is no further liability to tax on investors who are not higher-rate taxpayers at the time of the chargeable event unless what is known as the *top-sliced gain* on the sale of the investment bond, when added to the investor's other taxable income in that tax year, takes the investor's income into the higher-rate income tax band. This principle is explained further, below, using a worked example.

Top slicing

As noted above, accumulated gains on withdrawals in excess of the 5% cumulative allowance are potentially to higher-rate tax.

To establish whether a liability arises for investors who would otherwise be basic-rate taxpayers, the chargeable gain is divided by the number of complete years for which the investor has held the bond in order to arrive at, in effect, an average gain per policy year. This average gain is then treated as an extra slice of income to the investor and added for the purposes of this calculation on to the investor's other taxable income. If the total is still below the point at which taxable income is subject to higher rates of tax, there is no further tax to pay.

If, however, the addition of this extra slice of income pushes the individual over the threshold for higher rates of tax, the margin above the threshold is taxed at the additional rate noted above. The total tax due is then calculated by multiplying this figure by exactly the same number of years as was used in the initial top-slicing or averaging calculation – that is, the number of complete years the investment bond has been in force.

The calculation for encashments of only part of an investment bond holding is more complex, but the following example illustrates the tax treatment of encashment of a complete holding.

Example: Top slicing

An investor encashes a bond he has held for 5 years and 4 months, having invested £10,000 and encashing it for £30,000. His other taxable income is £1,000 below the threshold at which higher rate tax would be payable. Take the higher rate tax as being 17% higher than the basic rate of tax.

The calculation is as follows:

Divide the gain of £20,000 by the number of complete years the bond has been in force (5) = £4,000. Now, add this £4,000 to the investor's other taxable income. This indicates that £1,000 (25% of the divided gain) falls into the basic rate of tax and therefore suffers no further tax liability. The other £3,000 (75%) falls into the higher-rate tax band and suffers a further 17% tax. 17% of £3,000 = £510 and this figure is then multiplied by the number of complete years the bond has been in force: £510 × 5 = £2,550, and this is the additional income tax liability on the investment bond gain.

Even if the exact mathematical principles are difficult to grasp, the basic concept must be understood: higher-rate taxpayers will always be due to further tax liability, and basic-rate taxpayers (and even lower-rate and non-taxpayers) may suffer a liability if the divided gain takes their total taxable income into the higher-rate band.

PARTIAL WITHDRAWALS AND THE 5% ANNUAL ALLOWANCE

There is provision for the withdrawal of up to 5% of the initial investment each policy year without any immediate further liability to higher-rate income tax.

Any unused part of the 5% allowance can be carried forward to subsequent policy years so, for example, if there had been no withdrawals for the first six years, the allowance in the 7th policy year would be 35% of the initial investment. If withdrawals exceed the cumulative 5% allowance this is deemed to be a chargeable event on the excess amount, and there may therefore be an immediate liability to higher-rate tax upon some of the withdrawal.

This 5% withdrawal facility may be particularly attractive to higher-rate taxpayers requiring an income: they can enjoy what is, in effect, an income from the investment bonds by partial encashment of units that have, as described earlier, so far suffered internal tax of, probably, less than 20% on income and gains. They are, as the simplified example below demonstrates, apparently storing up a tax liability for the date on which they eventually encash the bonds but, if they can anticipate this might occur in a year in which they are not higher-rate taxpayers (even with the addition, of course, of the top-sliced gain) this liability may never materialize.

Example

An investor buys £100,000 of units in an investment bond. In the fourth year of the bond he encashes £20,000 while being a higher-rate taxpayer. No further tax liability arises under the 5% withdrawal facility

(4 x 5% of £100,000 = £20,000).

In the 11th policy year he encashes a further £50,000. He has already encashed £20,000 but the 5% facility allows a further £35,000 to be encashed without immediate further tax liability (i.e. 11 x 5% of £100,000 = £55,000, less £20,000 already withdrawn, equals £35,000).

In the 22nd policy year he encashes a further £45,000 of units. Again no further liability arises because his total encashments, in over 20 years, has not exceeded the original investment (20 years being the maximum accrual, of course, of 5%). Gains on all further encashments will now be potentially liable to higher-rate income tax.

TAXATION ON INCREMENTS TO EXISTING INVESTMENT BONDS

Investors should be aware that the practice among different insurance company providers of investment bonds is not identical with regard to the taxation treatment of additional investments to existing investment bonds.

With some insurance companies' investment bonds an additional investment (an *increment*) is treated for tax purposes as a new investment, even when added to the main policy and seemingly treated as an increment for internal purposes (such as sharing the same policy number). With other investment bonds an increment is treated for taxation as an increment. Although not perhaps immediately obvious, these two different ways in which the company views additional investments has a major affect upon the eventual tax treatment with important regard to the top-slicing calculation and the 5% withdrawal facility.

Example

Let us assume that John has effected a bond for £5,000 with Company A, and a similar amount with Company B and 15 years later is wishing to invest a further £95,000 to an existing bond.

Company A treats additional investments as increments for internal administration purposes, but the bond is worded in such a way that the increment is actually taxed as a new investment for taxation purposes.

Company B treats additional investments truly as increments to the original holding for both internal and taxation purposes.

Let us look at the different effects on the tax position as regards the cumulative 5% allowances and also upon final encashment 3 years later (i.e. after 18 years).

5% allowances

With Company A, the original investment would have accumulated allowances after 18 years of 5% of £5,000 for each whole year, giving a total accumulated allowance of 90% of £5,000 = £4,500. The new investment of £95,000 at that time would have only three years, allowance, i.e. 15% of £95,000, is £14,250. The total amount that may be withdrawn from the holding without immediate liability to higher rate tax is therefore £4,500 + £14,250 = £18,750.

With Company B the additional investment is deemed to have been made when the bond was originally effected, which means that both the original £5,000 and the additional £95,000 have 18 years' of 5% allowances. The maximum withdrawal that may be made from this investment without immediate liability to higher-rate tax is therefore 90% of £100,000 = £90,000: a huge difference over that available from Company A.

Top slicing

If, instead of partial encashment up to the 5% withdrawal limit, the investor encashed the total value of the bond after 18 years, the top slice calculation becomes potentially important for those individuals who are not higher-rate taxpayers on their other taxable income but may be pushed into the higher-rate band by the addition of the top-sliced gain on the investment bond.

Let us assume that the bond is now worth £120,000. Of this, £10,400 was from the first investment and £109,600 was from the later investment. Thus the total gain made is £120,000 less £100,000 = £20,000.

With Company A, the gain for top-slicing purposes is calculated by looking at the two investments independently. For the first investment of £5,000, the gain made is £5,400 and this is divided by 18 to arrive at a top-slice figure of £300. For the second investment, the gain made of £14,600 is divided by just 3 to arrive at a top-slice figure of £4,867. Thus the total top-slice addition to other taxable income is £5167. With Company B, the total investment of £100,000 is treated as a whole and therefore the gain is taken as a single figure of £20,000. This gain is divided by 18, to give a chargeable top slice of £1111 – a much lower figure than for Company A. John could quite conceivably save a substantial amount of higher-rate tax liability on the Company B investment as compared to Company A.

Without a doubt two of the major attractions to many investors of investment bonds is the 5% withdrawal facility and the top-slicing principle of tax liability on encashment. Many investors add further capital to existing bonds and so the author very strongly recommends investors and would-be investors in these vehicles to confirm whether the insurance company providers under consideration treat increments *for tax purposes* (not just for administrative purposes) as new investments or truly as increments. You may be surprised to find the number of insurance companies whose increments are deemed for tax purposes to be new investments.

APPROPRIATENESS OF INSURANCE INVESTMENT BONDS FOR AN INVESTOR

The primary advantage of insurance investment bonds is that they offer access to a collective investment arrangement and thus the benefits of diversification of investment risk and access to expert investment management. The range of funds available from many providers is sufficiently wide to accommodate most investor requirements.

Non-taxpayers and lower-rate taxpayers
Given that the underlying funds are subject to tax, irrecoverable by non-

taxpayers and lower-rate taxpayers, there is a distinct tax disadvantage within investment bonds for non-taxpayers. Other forms of collective investment offer similar degrees of diversification and professional fund management in a more tax-efficient way.

Basic-rate taxpayers

For basic-rate taxpayers, although not subject to further taxation on encashments (basic-rate tax being deemed to have been satisfied on the taxation within the fund), it could be argued that there is a still a tax penalty inherent in investment bonds because the life office pays tax on gains within the fund that currently many individual investors can avoid through their annual CGT exemptions.

However, the other taxation advantages within bonds could be seen to outweigh this potential disadvantage, including the 5% withdrawal facility and the top-slicing treatment of increments, for those taxpayers whose investment income might take them into the higher-rate tax band.

Other basic-rate taxpayers could be attracted to bonds for the switching facilities, range of funds, simplicity of operation or any combination of these, and other features, noted throughout this chapter.

Higher-rate taxpayers

For a higher-rate taxpayer this investment may offer an immediate form of partial tax shelter. If the bond can be managed in such a way as to avoid a chargeable event while the bondholder is a higher-rate taxpayer, and delayed until he or she may be a basic-rate tax payer (or even a non-taxpayer, which might occur particularly if he or she starts to live or work abroad for an extended period of time – see Chapter 17), liability to higher-rate tax on the gain may well be avoided.

Again, the decision as to whether to invest in this type of vehicle may be made partly or primarily on other grounds apart from taxation considerations (flexibility of investment, charges, etc.).

SUMMARY: INVESTMENT BONDS AND OTHER COLLECTIVE INVESTMENT VEHICLES

The broad similarities in taxation treatment of unit trusts, OEICs, investment trusts and (to a lesser extent) investment bonds means that the selection of the most appropriate vehicle or combination of vehicles will be determined in most cases by other factors, such as the level of charges (although there are less differences here than has been the case in the past), volatility and fund switching facilities.

The taxation treatment of investment bonds, though, differs from the other collective investment vehicles to such an extent that a fuller comparison for the situation of an individual investor should be made.

Overall, there is little doubt that collective investment vehicles, especially with falling levels of charges, should be considered as a core investment vehicle in most portfolios.

15 Individual Savings Accounts (ISAs)

INTRODUCTION

ISAs are a form of saving that was introduced in April 1999. They replaced two investment vehicles that were available up until that time called TESSAs (Tax Exempt Special Savings Accounts) and PEPs (Personal Equity Plans). Before looking at ISAs in more detail, it is worthwhile commenting upon the main features of these two types of vehicle – it can then be seen why and how ISAs take their current form. Moreover, both of those investment vehicles remain in force for existing investors for whom, obviously, ongoing features of these vehicles are still important.

TESSAS

TESSAs were special types of deposit-based account introduced in January 1991. They had to be held for five years to obtain the maximum tax advantage available. Broadly speaking, the interest that accumulates within a TESSA account does not suffer liability to income tax. This made them (and still makes them, for existing holders) particularly attractive to higher-rate taxpayers and (to a lesser extent) to basic-rate taxpayers. Depending upon the rate of interest as compared to alternative investment accounts, they could also be attractive to non-taxpayers. In fact, most deposit-taking institutions offer their highest rates on TESSAs, often quoting higher interest rates, even on such small deposits, than those available to investors with, say, more than £100,000 to invest outside of a TESSA.

The maximum amount that can be invested over the five years is limited to £9,000 per individual, with a maximum amount in any one year. This maximum amount is £1800 per annum, but with the provision that in the first year an investor could invest up to £3,000 (but then in the fifth year would be limited to just £600).

Accumulated *net* interest can be withdrawn during the five years, without effecting the tax shelter advantage, but if any of the capital is withdrawn the tax advantage of the account is lost.

If an investor has a maturing TESSA the capital content (but not the accrued interest) can be reinvested in an ISA in additional to the normal annual limit provided the transfer is made within six months of its maturity.

PEPS

Personal Equity Plans are also tax-sheltered investment vehicles, although of no fixed term. Income paid or accumulated within the PEP is free of liability to income tax, and capital growth is free of liability to capital gains tax. Of course, both of these features made PEPs (and, indeed, TESSAs) particularly attractive to higher-rate taxpayers – especially those who use their CGT allowance on a regular basis.

The maximum amount that could be invested in any tax year by an individual was limited to £6,000 in a *General PEP*, which could invest in unit trusts, investment trusts, shares or certain other securities. A further £3,000 could be invested in a *Single-Company PEP* investing, as the name implies, in the shares of one quoted company only (and therefore not, among other prohibited investments, in unit trusts or investment trusts).

For holdings in unit trusts and investment trusts to be permitted, the trust must have at least 50% of its holdings invested in UK or European Union equities.

A combination of TESSA and PEP allowance being used each year meant that an individual investor could accumulate substantial sums, over £10,000 each year, within a tax-exempt environment.

HOW ISAS REPLACED TESSAS AND PEPS

The main difference between the ISA and its (broadly) equally tax-favoured forerunners is that within just one investment medium an investor can invest in both deposit-type accounts and equities, either directly or through the medium of various investment vehicles including unit trusts, investment trusts and OEICs.

ISAs enjoy tax exemption on income and gains and may also, until tax year 2003/2004, reclaim the nominal 10% tax deemed to have been deducted at source from equity dividends.

As part of the aim to make investment vehicles more attractive to a wider cross section of the population the government has introduced a voluntary *kite mark*, called the CAT standard (standing for Charges, Access and Terms) for qualifying ISA providers to use to denote their compliance with the particular standards laid down by the government. It is important to note that meeting the CAT standards does not indicate in any way competitive interest rates or fund performance. More detail of the CAT standards is noted below.

ISAs are available at two different levels: the Maxi ISA and the Mini ISA.

MAXI ISA

Under the terms of a Maxi ISA the investor may hold a combination of different (approvable) investments, the most notable of which include stocks and shares (whether directly or through collective investment vehicles), life assurance-based investments and cash deposits. An ISA provider may provide only one or more, or indeed all, of these options within the same plan.

In any one tax year the maximum amount that can be invested is £5,000 (£7,000 in 1999/2000). Within this overall limit up to £1000 may be invested into cash deposits (£3,000 in 1999/2000), up to £1000 into life assurance-based investments, and £3,000 into stocks and shares. Alternatively up to £5,000 may be invested in stocks and shares with consequent reduced or nil allowances left for the others.

Unlike the PEP rule, there is no requirement for a minimum proportion of stocks and shares held within an ISA to be in UK or European holdings, although to meet the CAT standard an ISA *must* meet such a rule, very similar to the old PEP minimum.

In any one tax year, only one Maxi ISA can be effected and all investments within it must be through the same provider.

MINI ISA

With a Mini ISA an investor can choose to invest the cash entitlement with one ISA provider, the life assurance-based element with another, and the stocks and shares element with another.

The limits within each segment are the same as for ISAs generally: simply, the title describes the ISA offered by a provider who does not desire, or is not able, to offer investment opportunities within all the possible investment segments.

Without the Mini ISA facility an investor could not select an individual provider in each segment, not being able to contribute to more than one Maxi ISA in the same tax year.

MIXING MINI AND MAXI ISAS

It is not allowable for an investor to open both a Mini and a Maxi ISA in the same tax year. However, an investor could, if he or she so wished, choose to have a Mini ISA one year, and a Maxi ISA the following year, or vice versa.

WITHDRAWALS

ISAs are completely flexible as regards withdrawals. An investor can withdraw capital or interest from an ISA account without losing any of the tax benefits

147

accumulated up to that time. A partial withdrawal does not affect the tax sheltered environment for the remaining funds.

However, if an investor chooses to invest the full allowance into an ISA and, in the same year, wishes to withdraw some of the capital, he or she cannot then replace that capital in the same tax year within the ISA tax shelter.

Example

An investor has invested the full allowance of £5,000 and finds that he needs to withdraw £1,000. He cannot in the same tax year invest another £1,000 to 'reinstate' his £5,000 entitlement.

THE CAT STANDARDS

The main CAT standards are:

The cash element

- There should be no charges on the cash account. This means, for example, that if withdrawals can be made through a cash machine there should not be a charge for doing so. However, a provider is quite entitled to charge for replacing items already provided to an investor, such as duplicate statements.
- The minimum deposit or withdrawal allowed must not be more than £10 and withdrawals must be possible within 7 days.
- The margin between the interest rate payable and the Bank of England base rate must not exceed 2%. If the base rate moves upwards this must be reflected within a calendar month, although with downward movements the provider can take longer to adjust the rate as, obviously, the investor is not too concerned!

The stocks and shares element

- The total charges must not exceed 1% of the value of the underlying assets each year.
- The minimum single investment must not exceed £500 or, for monthly contributions, £50 a month.

- The investment fund must be at least 50% invested in European Union stocks and shares.
- There must not be any difference between the buying price and the selling price of the units (i.e. units must be 'single priced' (see Chapter 12).

It follows that an ISA that is not CAT kite-marked will for the stocks and shares element either have higher costs, higher minimum investments or withdrawals, a bid/offer spread, wider scope for a geographical spread of investment, or be invested more into gilts than equities.

RELEVANCE OF THE CAT KITE MARK

Because of the very low costs within CAT-marked ISAs, it is highly unlikely that providers could afford to give a full investment and advice service without levying additional fees or charges somewhere on the investor's portfolio.

For investors seeking more comprehensive advice, rather than just information, ISAs that are outside the CAT kite mark structure may well be appropriate if, for example, the ISA fails the CAT mark because of higher charges that are levied at least partially to pay for some degree of advice-giving.

TAXATION

Earlier in the chapter we outlined the taxation advantages of the forerunners to ISAs: TESSAs and PEPs. There are a number of differences between these vehicles and the taxation treatment of ISAs, being:

Interest on the cash element
This is added gross and free of tax (TESSAs: added net with the deducted tax added to the account at the end of the term unless some of the capital had been withdrawn from the account).

149

Dividends on shares

These are received by the ISA managers after deduction of income tax at the rate of 10%. As a concession until the end of the tax year starting April 2003 the managers will be able to reclaim that 10%, but not beyond that date.

When looking at the underlying investments of collective funds, those that have a high proportion in fixed-interest type investments such as gilts and corporate bonds have a tax benefit superior to those that are invested to a large degree in equities, where the income arises from dividends. However, it needs to be remembered that the long-term growth prospects from investments that are geared towards payment of interest are generally considered not as great as those linked more directly to equity growth. For the person who requires a high income return more than capital growth, this difference in taxation treatment of the income arising from underlying funds might be a determining factor in choosing the type of fund into which capital needs to be invested.

Life assurance element

The taxation rules for life assurance policies are not generally the same as for equities and deposit accounts. A life fund is liable for both capital gains tax and income tax on its underlying investments. Any part of a life fund that supports an ISA policy will have the income and capital growth arising on that part of the fund treated in the same way as interest and income arising on the cash and stocks and shares segments. This means that interest arising will be free of income tax, dividends arising will be subject to the usual 10% tax deduction (with the same concession as mentioned above until the expiry of the 2002-2003 tax year), and capital growth will be free of tax.

Furthermore, the investors themselves will receive all profits in their hands without the usual tax charges that can arise from the proceeds of life assurance policies, especially those related to higher-rate tax liability on a single capital investment.

In practical terms the life assurance elements provided within an ISA are likely to be single-premium investment plans rather than regular savings plans because these are normally designed to run for at least 10 years and, furthermore, have much higher costings than would normally be appropriate within an ISA.

SUMMARY: APPROPRIATENESS OF ISAS FOR AN INVESTOR

Non-taxpayers

Whether or not an ISA may be appropriate to an individual investor depends upon his or her investment objectives and tax position. For a non-taxpayer, the fact that income earned within an ISA is free of tax is of little relevance, although if the rate of interest on cash deposits within the ISA is higher than could be obtained on a normal gross earning account there is a clear argument for investing through the ISA route. Moreover, where there is a possibility of becoming a taxpayer at a future date, investing in the ISA has attractions in building up deposits that are already sheltered from potential tax.

Taxpayers

There is little doubt that the vast majority of taxpayers should seriously consider ISAs as one of, if not the main, fundamental parts of their portfolio, however modest in size for larger-scale investors. Low charges (at least potentially) and a wide range of investment opportunities make it hard to see why the take up of ISAs has not been significantly greater than has so far been the case.

16 Pensions

INTRODUCTION

The various investments reviewed in the previous chapters have been capital investments that provide for either income, or capital growth, or a mix of both.

An investment vehicle that is completely different to those looked at so far and has many taxation attractions is the pension scheme.

There are many different types of pension scheme in the UK – a range well beyond the scope of this book – and so we concentrate in this chapter on the benefits from *money purchase* or *defined contribution* pension schemes. These pension schemes, whether under occupational or personal pension legislation, accumulate a fund which, when the benefits start to be taken, may generally be taken partly as a tax-free lump sum (except Additional Voluntary Contributions – AVCs – and Free Standing AVCs), but mostly must be used to buy an annuity.

In planning the outline for this book a number of people have expressed surprise to me at the inclusion of pension schemes on the basis that 'if the book is about investments, why are you talking about pensions?'. However, what is a pension scheme if not simply an investment fund with a specific tax 'wrap-around'?

Fundamentally, therefore, we are looking in this chapter not at the technical details of the various types of pension scheme, but at the investment strategies that may be followed within a pension scheme where the investor has control over the investment fund (in other words, in almost all schemes other than final salary schemes).

BENEFITS OF A PENSION PLAN

The main benefits that may be provided from a pension arrangement include:

- benefits may start to be taken at any age from 50 to 75.
- tax relief is granted on contributions at the contributor's highest marginal rate of income tax.
- capital gains and income accumulated within the fund are free of capital gains tax and free of income tax, although tax deducted at source on dividends cannot be reclaimed.
- benefits can usually be taken partly as a tax-free lump sum, although the remainder must be used to buy a (taxable) lifetime annuity.

WHEN BENEFITS CAN BE TAKEN

The age at which benefits may be taken from a pension plan depends to some extent upon the type of pension scheme. Generally, though, benefits may be taken at any age from 50 but benefit payments must start no later than age 75.

With personal pensions there is no requirement for the individual to retire to enable him or her to start drawing the benefits and, even when retired, there is no requirement to start to draw the benefits. Thus the personal pension may be not be seen simply as a retirement benefits scheme but alternatively (or additionally) as a potentially tax-efficient investment vehicle with restricted maturity dates.

The conditions under which benefits may be taken from occupational pension schemes are more restrictive (generally a member must formally retire to draw the benefits and, when he or she does retire, the pensioner will usually be obliged to start to draw those benefits) but still the flexibility between the ages of 50 and 75 remains, albeit usually with the consent of the scheme's trustees.

In recent years, options have been designed that enable an investor in a personal pension contract to start to take benefits in stages. This gives added flexibility (although usually with added charges) to plan the 'phasing-in' of benefits from pension schemes. Much more discussion and detail of these strategies forms part of a sister book to this publication, *Retirement Income Planning*, but further discussion is beyond the scope of this book.

TAX RELIEF ON CONTRIBUTIONS

The initial advantage of a pension plan as an investment is that contributions made into a tax-approved scheme (the vast majority of pension schemes – both individual and group – fall into this category) attract tax relief at the investor's highest marginal rate of income tax. By an Inland Revenue concession am employee effecting a personal pension, under which contributions are paid net of basic-rate tax relief, obtains the benefit of that relief even if not a taxpayer.

This advantage can be viewed by the investor in one of two particular ways: either a refund of part of the contribution or as a grossing-up of the net contribution.

Example: refund of tax from gross pension contribution

A higher-rate tax payer makes a gross pension contribution of £1,000 in a particular tax year. Subject to at least £1,000 of taxable income falling within the 40% band he or she will – usually by an amendment to the tax code (i.e. his personal allowances) – receive a refund of £400, making the net contribution only £600 even though £1,000 is invested in the pension fund.

Example – grossing up of a net pension contribution

An investor in very similar circumstances decides that he wants to contribute £1,000 to his pension scheme and does not want to separately benefit from the tax relief on contributions. He can therefore consider investing £1,666 to his pension scheme because, after tax relief at 40% (subject to at least £1,666 of his taxable income falling in to the higher rate band), his net contribution will be £1,000.

Whichever way the investor considers the pension contribution, the advantage of tax relief on contributions is particularly attractive to higher-rate taxpayers, although still highly attractive to basic-rate taxpayers.

ACCUMULATION OF CAPITAL IN A TAX-SHELTERED ENVIRONMENT

Pension funds are not liable to pay tax on any income or gains made within the fund (with some very minor exceptions), although they cannot reclaim tax deemed to have been deducted at source from company dividends.

This advantage of having capital appreciate within an environment where the accumulating fund obtains some shelter from tax becomes greater the longer the fund has to accumulate. In other words, the younger an individual starts to make significant contributions to a pension fund the greater will be the benefit of this taxation advantage (although noting that the fund cannot usually be drawn upon until the investor's age 50, as noted above).

TAX-FREE CASH

Within certain limits, from most types of pension scheme it is possible to take part of the pension fund, at the date benefits are taken, as a tax-free cash sum (additional voluntary contributions are the notable exception). Bearing in mind that tax relief has already been granted on the investment initially made, and the accumulating fund has been largely tax exempt (with the notable exception of the inability to reclaim tax deducted from company dividends), this is a valuable concession and one which it is rumoured could be removed by a brave future chancellor of the exchequer.

INCOME

Any remaining fund after the tax-free cash has been taken is used to provide an income. This income is payable for life and is guaranteed either as regards its amount or as to the method of calculating the amount payable (in the case of escalating pensions) on a year-by-year basis.

Example

John Smith reaches his retirement age at 60 and starts to take the benefits from his accumulated personal pension fund of £100,000. He takes full advantage of the ability to take the maximum of £25,000 as a tax-free lump sum.

His remaining fund of £75,000 must be used to provide an annuity income.

Let us assume that his annuity income rate obtainable based on his age is calculated by the insurance company offering the annuity at £6%. This would provide him with an income throughout the rest of his life of £4,500 per annum (i.e. 6% of £75,000 = £4,500), taxable as earned income.

If he preferred that the income increased in payment each year then the starting level of income would be lower. The table below gives an idea of the level of reduction that could occur, in contrast to the level pension. Note that these figures are subject to (sometimes rapid) change depending mostly on the level of prevailing market interest rates.

Rate of Increase in Income	Annual Income
Nil	£4,500 per annum
3% per annum	£3,350 per annum
5% per annum	£3,000 per annum

Retirement income options can frequently be complex, and are beyond the scope of this book . They are, though, detailed and discussed in a sister book in this series.

THE OVERALL EFFECT

It is possible to play about with combinations of percentages to achieve almost any result vested interests might care to demonstrate, but an indisputable total effect of the taxation concession granted to pension schemes is the combined advantage of tax relief on contributions and the largely tax-exempt treatment of the accumulating fund.

This combination is particularly attractive to higher-rate taxpayers. As a very simple example (ignoring, perhaps dangerously, charges under the respective investment vehicles):

Example

Investor A, a 40% taxpayer, invests £10,000 net into a pension fund, which represents a £16,667 grossed-up contribution. His fund grows at a gross rate – untaxed, of course – of 10%, indicate a doubling-up of his £16,667 fund about every seven years.

Investor B, also a 40% taxpayer, invests £10,000 into an investment vehicle with no tax concessions. His fund grows at 10% gross and is accordingly subjected to tax at 40%, thus indicating a net rate of growth of 6%. This fund, starting at only £10,000 (as opposed to £16,667 in the pension scheme) doubles in value only every twelve years or so (7 years in a pension scheme).

It does not take an accomplished mathematician to identify the advantage the pension scheme has over its less tax-favoured counterpart!

COMPARABLE INVESTMENT VEHICLES

The tax-sheltered accumulation of profits is similar to that provided under an ISA, but an ISA does not have the advantage of the tax relief on money invested. The ISA does, however, have the advantage that all the fund can be withdrawn as a lump sum at any time; pension scheme monies cannot be taken until a minimum age and then can in only rare circumstances be taken entirely as a lump sum.

There has been considerable discussion and argument in determining which of these two investment vehicles is, overall, the most tax efficient, bearing in mind these contrasting tax benefits. The author, although loath to appear to be sitting on the fence, concludes it is very much 'horses for courses' and the respective advantages will benefit different people in different circumstances.

For most people, investment in both vehicles is likely to be advisable.

SUMMARY

Where a part of an investment portfolio can comfortably and confidently be committed to the investor's age 50 or beyond, and especially where the investor is a basic- or higher-rate taxpayer, directing part of the portfolio to pension contributions must be seriously considered.

The investor at his or her peril divorces the concepts of pension contributions from a non-pension investment portfolio: they should and must form part of the same strategy.

17 Offshore Investment

SCOPE OF THIS CHAPTER

Definition: investing 'offshore'
Investments made in countries outside of the UK. Note, though, Jersey and the Isle of Man, having different taxation structures from the UK, are deemed offshore for these purposes. For maximum taxation planning opportunities, the offshore investment offices are invariably situated within the jurisdiction of countries with highly favourable taxation treatment of these investments (in fact, usually levying no taxation).

Just as the *detailed* practice regarding residence, ordinary residence and domicile arguably affect relatively small numbers of investors and so are beyond the scope of this book, so the *detailed* vagaries of offshore investing, particularly as regards strategies using trusts, are also outside the aim of this chapter.

Instead, we concentrate here on *fundamental* investment and portfolio strategies appropriate to the largest numbers of investors – those who are resident, ordinarily resident and domiciled in the UK. For brevity we will call them, in this chapter, 'Brits at home'. For the purposes of identifying the appropriateness or otherwise of different forms of offshore investing we can identify four other categories of potential investor, being:

- 'Brits abroad';
- 'Brits planning to go abroad';
- 'Foreigners in the UK';
- 'Foreigners abroad'.

These other categories of investor are beyond the scope of this book, although we shall briefly outline the potential attractions of offshore investing for each of them towards the end of this chapter.

To understand the implications of portfolio planning for these various categories, it is first of all necessary to understand the meaning of three particular aspects of an individual's circumstances:

159

- country of residence;
- country of ordinary residence;
- country of domicile.

Very simply, these three terms identify the country in which the individual now lives (country of residence), usually lives (country of ordinary residence) and was born or now permanently lives or expects to live in (country of domicile). In particular the last definition is over-simple, but will suffice for our immediate purposes in this book.

In the first part of this chapter we look a little more closely at the definitions of residence and domicile, and identify into which of the above four categories an investor may fall, helping us to identify appropriate offshore investment vehicles, if any.

In the second part we look at the main types of offshore investment and divide these into two convenient categories which then dictate not only the taxation treatment of the investments but also the appropriateness for investors in one of the four situations listed above.

RESIDENCE AND DOMICILE

Introduction to the principles of residence and domicile

Quite apart from the importance to an individual's liability to UK income taxes generally, the principles of residence, ordinary residence and domicile are vital in determining whether, or to what extent, an individual might benefit from holding some or all of his or her investment portfolio *offshore*.

As an initial indication of the importance of these concepts, an individual who is neither UK resident nor UK ordinarily resident should seriously consider moving most or all of the portfolio offshore, whether or not he or she is also UK domiciled. An individual who is not UK domiciled will or should similarly favour offshore investments even if he or she is both resident and ordinarily resident in the UK. An individual who is domiciled, resident and ordinarily resident in the UK might not, at least on the face of it, benefit from the attractions of investing offshore to the same extent as the first two categories of investor I have just mentioned but, as I discuss later, there could still be some very exciting opportunities.

So, how can it be determined whether an individual is taxable as being:

a) UK resident;
b) UK ordinarily resident;
c) UK domiciled?

UK resident

With two particular exceptions an individual will be taxed, or not taxed, as a UK resident for the whole of a particular tax year. It cannot therefore be the case that an individual can consider himself (or herself) a UK resident for two months while living in this country, then a non-resident for the next two weeks while on holiday in Spain, then a UK resident again for the next two months back in this country, and so on. Depending on the application of the residency rules he or she will be taxed as if a UK resident for the whole of the tax year in question, or for none of it.

It is important to note that the term 'UK resident' is not determined in any legislation and so to identify the rules applied by the Inland Revenue we have to look primarily at the Inland Revenue booklet: *IR20: Residents and Non-residents – Liability to Tax in the United Kingdom.*

The 'six month' rule
If an individual is in the UK for at least six months (for these purposes at least 183 days, but days of departure from, or arrival in, the UK are not counted) in a given tax year, he or she will definitely be taxed as a UK resident for that year. The Inland Revenue stresses that there will be no exceptions to this rule.

The 'three month' rule
If an individual visits the UK regularly and after four tax years the visits during these years have averaged three months (for this purpose 91 days) then that person will be treated as resident from the fifth year, although there are exceptions to this general ruling. These exceptions can either cause an individual

161

INVESTMENT PORTFOLIO PLANNING

to be deemed resident earlier or later than the general time period of 'after four years'.

Exceptions to the 'complete tax year' residency rule

It was noted, above, that an individual will usually be taxed as a UK resident or non-resident for the whole of a tax year. Two exceptions to this principle apply: emigration and longer-term working abroad.

Emigration and longer-term working abroad

If an individual can demonstrate that he or she is leaving this country permanently, or with the intention of permanency, then he or she will be taxed as a UK resident up to and including the day of departure from the UK, and then treated as a non-resident from the following day.

Dual residence

So far we have outlined only the rules used by the UK in determining whether or not an individual will be liable to certain taxes in this country. You should note that it is possible for an individual to be taxed as a UK resident for the whole of a tax year in which he or she has actually spent only a relatively short period in this country. Although it is a long way beyond the scope of this book, it is worth noting and remembering that other countries also apply rules to determine their equivalent of 'residency' and, some of those countries having rules similar to our own, a number of people have more than one country of residence in certain years.

This being the case it can be noted that they may therefore be liable to tax, on the same income or gains, in more than one country. This would of course be patently unfair and so the UK has agreed special rules with most countries to ensure that an individual in these circumstances will not be unfairly treated.

UK ordinarily resident

There is no reliable definition of being *ordinarily resident*, but the Inland Revenue publication IR20 describes it, rather unhelpfully, as being 'broadly equivalent to habitually resident'. Certainly we know that a person who is considered resident in the UK under the three-month rule (see above) will also be considered ordinarily resident.

A great deal of discretion is therefore attached to this definition – mostly in the hands of the Inland Revenue. It is an important distinction to make, though, especially as an individual who is considered resident but not ordinarily resident in the UK has certain offshore investment taxation planning opportunities unavailable. For our 'Brits at home', though, this should not present too many complications.

UK domicile

Domicile of origin
Under UK law (as this is not a common concept around the world) an individual acquires a country of domicile on the day he or she is born – this being the country of domicile of the father. It is irrelevant where the child is born, as is the country of the mother's domicile (unless the child is illegitimate). This is known as the individual's *domicile of origin* and stays with that person throughout life.

Domicile of dependence
Before a child is able, in law, to acquire a different country of domicile – the domicile of choice (see below) – if the domicile of the relevant parent changes then the child's country of domicile also changes, this now becoming known as the child's domicile of dependence. Note that the child's domicile of origin does not change, but the domicile of dependence overrides his domicile of origin for UK taxation purposes. In the UK (outside Scotland) this continues till the child is age 16 (in Scotland, 12 for girls and 14 for boys).

Domicile of choice
This describes the country in which an individual intends to live for the foreseeable long-term future – possibly for the rest of his or her life. The description relates not to the choice of the taxpayer, whose intentions will be surmised from the nature of his or her actions, as outlined below, but to the choice of the Inland Revenue – it is they who decide the country of domicile

of choice for a taxpayer.

This often causes confusion and arguments between taxpayers and the Inland Revenue, but to give some indication of the issues the Inland Revenue take into account in determining the individual's country of domicile:

- where the individual's children are being educated;
- how long the individual has lived in the country;
- ownership of a home in the country, and/or in a previous country of residence;
- business activities in the country, and/or in other countries;
- the country in which a will has been effected, indicating the country in which the individual foresees dying.

None of these issues indicates conclusive proof of the country of domicile; they are all taken into account only as indicators.

The most important aspect of the individual's country of *domicile of choice* is that where it is different from the individual's domicile of origin or domicile of dependence, the domicile of choice overrides the others for UK taxation purposes.

Deemed domicile

This concept relates only to the inheritance tax position of the investor which, though important, is beyond the scope of this book. Broadly it means that an individual can be liable to IHT as a UK domicile even though not falling into one of the categories noted above if he or she has lived in this country for an extended period of time.

DEFINING OUR FIVE MAIN CATEGORIES OF INVESTOR

Now, bringing together these states of residence and domicile, the following broad categorizations can be outlined:

'Brits at home'

UK resident, ordinarily resident, and domiciled. The main category for the remainder of this chapter.

'Brits abroad'
Not UK resident, and usually not UK ordinarily resident. UK domiciled. These people can potentially benefit from favourable investment taxation opportunities in offshore investments during the time they are abroad, if for an extended period.

'Brits planning to go abroad'
All the above at present, but planning or expecting for one or more of them to change at some stage in the future (usually, at least, the country of residence and ordinary residence). As we discuss later, these people might profitably invest offshore in anticipation of favourable taxation treatment following their departure from the UK.

'Foreigners in the UK'
UK resident but not UK domicile. Usually also UK ordinarily resident. These people can profitably invest offshore, especially if they anticipate not remaining in the UK for the rest of their lives.

'Foreigners abroad'
Neither UK resident nor ordinarily resident nor UK domiciled. Mostly, these people will be subject entirely to the taxation regime of their own country (or the country in which they are living at the time). This is well beyond the scope of this book.

Now, we start to look at how 'Brits at home' in particular, but some of the other categories (in passing), might benefit from investing offshore.

OFFSHORE INVESTMENT VEHICLES

The range of offshore investment vehicles

The main categories of offshore investment vehicles we shall consider in this chapter are:

- distributor funds;
- non-distributor funds;
- offshore bank and other deposit accounts; and
- offshore investment bonds.

Distributor funds

These are offshore funds that, as the name implies, distribute all (or the largest part) of income and gains accruing to the fund on a regular basis. There are conditions that determine whether a fund has distributor or non-distributor (see below) status.

Distributor funds offer little or no benefit to 'Brits at home' (indeed, they can even bring adverse taxation implications for these people) because they are in general taxed in the same way as a UK-based unit trust. They may be attractive to other categories of investor but, as noted earlier, these are beyond the scope of this book and so, while stressing their potential attractions elsewhere, we are largely discounting them from further discussion here.

Non-distributor funds

These, again as the name clearly implies, do not distribute income or gains to investors, instead 'rolling-up' those profits within the fund itself. A common alternative title to non-distributor funds – *gross roll-up funds* – clearly indicates the taxation treatment within the fund: there is no immediate liability to tax but a liability in the hands of the investor arises when the funds are withdrawn. This does not mean to say that the investor *will* incur liability to UK income tax – as we discuss in the next part of this chapter that will depend on the status of the investor, in turn dictating whether there is a potential liability to UK taxation in general.

Offshore bank and deposit accounts

These accounts work in exactly the same way as their onshore equivalents, although, depending on the institution with which the account is held, access to the money may not be so immediate (although it usually is). Furthermore the investor may find a little more difficulty identifying an offshore account with a cheque book facility.

'Brits at home' are taxed on income on these accounts in the tax year in which it arises, whether or not that income or the underlying capital is transferred to the UK. This liability, broadly matching the liability on UK-based savings accounts, stresses that no taxation advantage is gained by leaving the account monies offshore – the income will be taxed more or less immediately, anyhow.

As with distributor funds, these accounts have attractions for taxpayers falling into a category other than 'Brits at home' and thus, although important to those other categories, no further discussion is contained in this chapter.

Offshore investment bonds

The principle behind these bonds is very similar to that behind *onshore* investment bonds insofar, first of all, that they are *collective* investment vehicles that invite individual investors to buy units in a fund (or, with most offshore investment providers, a *range* of funds), thereby gaining access to professional and (hopefully) expert fund management in a cost-effective way.

There, however, is where the similarities end. The most important and striking difference between the onshore and offshore investment bonds is the taxation treatment within the bond on accumulating income and gains: the onshore bond is subject to taxation (technically and broadly at the rate of 20%, but in practice often 2% or 3% lower than this figure), whereas the offshore investment bond suffers no immediate liability to tax on the increasing value. The *quid pro quo* of this seemingly favourable tax treatment of the offshore version is that, on encashment (or, more technically, on the happening

167

of the chargeable event – see below for a list and brief explanation of *chargeable events),* the whole of the accumulated gain within the offshore version is subject to income tax in the hands of the bond holder at that time. This contrasts with the onshore bond under which there is no further liability to UK taxation where the bond holder at encashment is not a higher-rate tax payer (see Chapter 14 for a more precise discussion of these points).

Implications and uses of these offshore investment vehicles

The attractions or otherwise of one or more these vehicles for investors in different residency and domicile situations will become much clearer in the final part of this chapter, but to summarize the tax positions of the four investments at this initial stage:

Distributor funds	Immediate liability to income tax as the distribution is made.
Non-distributor funds	No immediate liability to UK income tax on the rolled-up gain, but liability arises on withdrawals.
Offshore bank accounts	Immediate liability to tax as the income arises.
Investment bonds	No immediate liability to tax on the increasing value of the bond units, but full liability to UK income tax on a chargeable event.

You will see, then, that *distributor funds* and *offshore bank accounts* are taxed in very similar ways to each other, and n*on-distributor funds* and offshore *investment bonds* are also taxed in very similar ways to each other.

It is the latter group of investments – investment bonds and non-distributor funds – which, being potentially appropriate to 'Brits at home', are now considered in more depth for the remainder of this chapter.

OFFSHORE INVESTING FOR 'BRITS AT HOME'

Taxation treatment of the investor

These individuals are liable to UK income tax on income arising *anywhere in the world* as and when that income arises. This applies to both earned and unearned (i.e. investment) income, and the liability arises – it must be stressed – whether or not the income is remitted to the UK. This means, for example, that income arising on offshore bank or other deposit accounts will be taxed as it arises offshore, with the same principles applying to dividends on offshore investments and (less commonly in investment portfolios) rental income on offshore or overseas property.

As regards capital gains tax (CGT) very similar principles apply in that the 'Brits at home' is liable to CGT on capital gains made anywhere in the world and, again, the liability arises as the gain arises, whether or not the proceeds from that gain are remitted to the UK.

By imposing these income tax and CGT rules the Inland Revenue ensure that 'Brits at home' cannot avoid or even materially delay a liability to UK income tax by structuring a portfolio outside the UK but, as we discuss below, there are a significant number of these individuals who *could* benefit from having part or all of their investment portfolio overseas – for convenience usually in an offshore investment vehicle.

Before discussing the possible attractions of investing offshore for these individuals, for the sake of completeness we should also note the situation regarding inheritance tax (IHT).

If an individual is domiciled in the UK then he or she will be potentially liable to IHT on transfers of assets wherever in the world those assets are (or were, prior to the transfer) situated. It is convenient and straightforward to note the similar tax treatments between income tax, CGT and IHT with the important and primary difference between the three taxes being the individual's country of residence and ordinary residence (which affects income tax and CGT) and the individual's country of domicile (which affects IHT as well as income tax and CGT). There is, you should be aware, the principle of *deemed domicile* under which an individual can be *deemed* to be domiciled in the UK *for IHT purposes only*, if he or she was either *domiciled* in the UK within the three years immediately preceding the relevant time (that is, the relevant date of transfer) or if he or she was *resident* in the UK in not less than seventeen out of the twenty income tax years ending with the tax year in which the relevant time falls (the relevant time broadly being the date of transfer of the assets). The concept of *deemed domicile*, you should particularly note, is relevant only to liability to IHT and not relevant to income tax or CGT and therefore, with the exception of estate planning (which, in any depth, is beyond the scope of this book), is not a concept relevant to portfolio planning in the sense we have been describing in previous chapters.

Now let us look at the four main types of offshore investment to identify and quantify the potential taxation advantages for 'Brits at home'.

Non-distributor funds for 'Brits at home'

These funds distribute less than 85% of their annual income (i.e. profit), therefore accruing a value within the fund (often known as a *gross roll-up* fund) with no immediate liability to UK taxation, even for those individuals who are currently UK resident, ordinarily resident and domiciled.

The liability to UK taxation for these individuals is not, however, avoided altogether: it is *deferred*, and continues to be deferred until withdrawals are made from the fund, at which time liability to UK income tax arises on the calculated gain on that part of the fund withdrawn. The rules for the calculation of the gain on a withdrawal of only a part of the value of the non-distributor fund are a little complex and beyond the scope of this book. Suffice to say that the liability is to income tax at the individual's highest marginal rate at the time of the withdrawal, with no allowance for indexation relief or annual CGT exemption because the gain is technically deemed to be one of income (simply, income that has not previously been withdrawn) rather than a capital gain.

Non-distributor funds can indeed have their uses in portfolio planning for 'Brits at home', particularly for those who can anticipate their highest marginal rate of income tax falling between the date the investment in the fund is made and the date of withdrawal. This is because, during that interim period, the investor will avoid immediate liability to income tax (which would, for example, be at the 40% – highest rate), deferring the liability until such time as he or she is a basic-rate taxpayer or, perhaps, even a non-taxpayer. These individuals are quite commonplace, particularly those with earned and investment income not greatly into the higher-rate tax bands who can foresee a reduction in their earned income at retirement will drop them into a lower tax band.

Non-distributor funds, then, should be considered for all taxpayers – especially higher-rate tax payers – who can foresee a future fall in income, noting that withdrawal at a time when their highest marginal rate of tax has *not* fallen will simply (or in most cases simply) result in a *tax neutral* outcome – they have avoided higher-rate tax on the accumulation of the profit only to pay exactly the same rate of tax on eventual withdrawal from the fund.

Similar tax treatment to non-distributor funds applies also to offshore investment bonds, but the latter investment vehicle has additional advantages for those seeking the flexibility of making occasional withdrawals of part of their offshore investment without immediate liability to UK income tax.

Offshore investment bonds for 'Brits at home'

Offshore investment bonds accumulate gains – both income and capital gains – internally with no immediate liability to UK taxation either on the fund or on the investor (with the exception of withholding tax on certain investments, being non-reclaimable tax deducted at source, such as the taxation on dividends in the UK).

However, as with non-distributor funds, the liability to UK tax is not completely avoided, it is *deferred*. It is deferred, in fact, until such time as a *chargeable event* occurs. This bond being non-qualifying (just as its *onshore* equivalent), the range of chargeable events is quite broad, being:

- death;
- maturity;
- surrender;
- certain *part* surrenders (see below);
- policy loan;
- assignment for money or moneys worth.

Thus on the happening of any of these events the gain within the bond is deemed to have been realized (at least in part, as regards those part surrenders) and a charge to UK income tax arrives immediately on the bond holder on the whole of that gain. As with non-distributor funds, the liability is to income tax and not, as one might imagine from the apparent nature of the profit, a charge to CGT. Thus no CGT reliefs or exemptions are available and the whole of the gain is subject to income tax at the bond holder's highest marginal rate of income tax.

The potential uses of these offshore investment bonds can, it should be obvious from our discussion of non-distributor funds, be identified as tax deferral for individuals who expect or anticipate their highest marginal rate of tax to fall in the period leading up to the chargeable gain.

Offshore deposit accounts and distributor funds for 'Brits at home'

These provide little or no benefit over their onshore equivalents, as noted already, and so will not be considered further.

Offshore investing: of limited application?

You should, first of all, be aware that offshore investing does not mean restricting the range of investment options; the same range of asset classes as exists for onshore investments also exists for offshore investments. Indeed, a number of offshore providers who are part of much larger financial services groups offer exactly the same investment funds offshore as onshore, meaning that overall investment performance (before charges and taxation differences are considered) will be exactly the same offshore as onshore.

Offshore investing for 'Brits at home': a summary

For individuals who are UK resident, ordinarily resident and domiciled and who do not expect their highest marginal rate of tax to fall between the date the investment is made and the eventual date of 'encashment', that is, withdrawal from a non-distributor fund or chargeable event with an offshore investment fund, then offshore investing may have little obvious appeal unless, for example, the individual can anticipate immigration abroad or an extended period of work abroad at some future date.

For individuals with this residency and domicile status who *can*, though, anticipate a future fall in their highest marginal rate of tax, offshore investing may well have attractions, probably favouring the offshore investment bond over non-distributor funds unless there are sound reasons to the contrary.

It should in any event be apparent that individuals with this residence and domicile status cannot hope to benefit, except perhaps by the merest amount of tax deferral, by investing in either offshore distributor funds or in offshore banks or other deposit accounts.

A final risk warning!

We very strongly recommend that investors always seek and obtain specialist and personalized professional advice relating to their own circumstances and requirements before seriously considering investments in general, and offshore investments in particular.

Index